YOU CAN'T FIX DEAD

The Physical Change and Spiritual Transformation of Travis McNeil

CHRIS M. SCHWAB

YOU CAN'T FIX DEAD
Copyright © 2015 by Chris M. Schwab

Names may have been changed to protect individuals' identities.

Unless otherwise indicated, all scripture quotations taken from the New American Standard Bible®, Copyright © 1960, 1962, 1963, 1968, 1971, 1972, 1973, 1975, 1977, 1995 by The Lockman Foundation. Used by permission. Scripture quotations marked (ESV) are from the ESV® Bible (The Holy Bible, English Standard Version®), copyright © 2001 by Crossway, a publishing ministry of Good News Publishers. Used by permission. All rights reserved. The Living Bible copyright © 1971 by Tyndale House Foundation. Used by permission of Tyndale House Publishers Inc., Carol Stream, Illinois 60188. All rights reserved.

Printed in Canada

ISBN: 978-1-4866-1196-6

Word Alive Press
131 Cordite Road, Winnipeg, MB R3W 1S1
www.wordalivepress.ca

Cataloguing in Publication may be obtained through Library and Archives Canada

I began by asking Tammy why she had never asked me about Jesse's mother. She said that she didn't care about who she was. I then told her that I was Jesse's mother.

She didn't seem to understand, so I started at my birth as Tanya Elizabeth McNeil and related my history, including my feelings growing up, to the start of hormone therapies and surgeries. I tried to squeeze as much of my life as possible into a short period of time.

"Before you say anything. I'll understand if you want to break up, and I promise not to have any hard feelings." When I finally ran out of things to say, I asked, "Do you have any questions?"

Tammy was silent for a long period of time.

"It doesn't matter," she said. "I enjoy being around the person you are now, not the person you used to be."

Then she leaned over and kissed me.

CONTENTS

ACKNOWLEDGEMENTS

by Travis McNeil

First, let me say thank you for your interest in reading this book. It is my hope that you will be blessed by not only knowing a brief story about me and all the things I have been through in my life that brought me to where I am today, but that you will gain an understanding that God can use *anybody!* If He can use a guy like me, He can surely use someone like you.

Thank you to my mom and dad. You both are with the Lord now, but I was so blessed and honoured to have you as my parents. Through a great many challenges, neither of you ever made me feel unloved or unwanted. You loved me in the best ways possible, and for that I am so very grateful. I am the man I am because I had the parents I had! I love and miss you both each and every day.

A special thank you to Chris Schwab for your gentle and patient nature while we went through lots of tea and coffee, and the many hours listening to me and taking notes—even when I couldn't remember some details or had gotten details mixed up. The journey was both terrifying and healing. The friendship that has developed between us will forever be unshakable.

A few friends have walked this crazy walk with me and have loved and supported me through it all. I want to give them each a shout-out.

- To my sisters Selena and Jamie: I think we could all write a book about our lives. I love you both very much. You are never far from my thoughts and always in my prayers. I am proud to say you are my sisters even if you guys still owe me about a case of chocolate bars!

- To my wife Tammy: thank you for sticking by my side through thick and thin, through sickness and in health, for richer and poorer, good and bad! You are an amazing lady who I'm blessed to have with me, going through this crazy thing we call life. Although we have had our fair share of struggles, I know I can grab a hold of your hand and we can face it together and always come out stronger. Together until the end! I love you!

- To my son Jesse: even when you drive me crazy, I am so proud of you and the man you are becoming. Thank you for loving me and supporting me through all my craziness, too.

- To all my stepchildren: Melissa and Mailyn, although the relationship between your mother and I didn't work out, I love you both and I am honoured to have the privilege of still having you both in my life. You truly are a blessing to me! Carrissa, Cassandra, Angela, and Dustin: I am honoured to be your stepdad; you all challenge me and encourage me to be a better person each and every day. I love you all! A special thank you to Melissa, Jesse, and Carrissa for my beautiful grandchildren! Andrew, Nathan, Haeleigh, Peyton, Maddison, Ben, and Lukacs: Papa loves you all to the moon and back several times.

- To Ervin and Byra: you both have been an enormous part of my life since I decided to start over in Calgary. We have been through the good, the bad, and the ugly together. But at the end of the day, I know who I can call! You guys are not just friends, you are my family.

- To Papa Sam and Mama Linda: a guy couldn't ask for better friends, mentors, or spiritual parents. You have been so loving and supportive of me and my family. I love you both so very much! I'm not sure I could have done it without your guidance, love, and support. I am grateful that the Lord brought you into my life.

- To all the members of my church, especially Pastor Jill, the congregation members at my home church, and the teachers at the Bible College. Thank you for being a true example of the love Jesus demonstrated, by loving the unlovable! I am so blessed and honoured and grateful for each and every one of you. You bring enrichment to my life every time I encounter you.

- Most of all, thank you to my Lord and Saviour, Jesus Christ, for loving me in spite of myself. I thank you for giving me the family you blessed me with. I also thank you for the church family you called me to, and for providing me with everything I have.

I wish I could have listed everybody who has been through this crazy life with me, but that would make the acknowledgements longer than the book! Just know that each and every one of you hold a special place in my heart. Never doubt that I love you, but that love pales in comparison to the love the Lord Jesus has for you! May each and every one of you be showered with love and blessings.

INTRODUCTION

Have you ever reached a time in your life when you had no hope for the future? Do you know what it feels like to plan the end of your life?

I'm going to introduce you to a man who has been to that place in his life many times over but today is living a life filled with hope. Travis has come to know the truth that has answered man's greatest need. When you know this truth, you will have the inner strength to face and overcome any obstacle in your life.

What follows is a story of pain, confusion, destruction, and in the end redeeming love. This is a true recording of what someone will suffer as a result of their wrong decisions. You will read about all the ways a person can pursue peace, but never seem to find it. The beginning of this story is a search for identity, and the end of this story is the discovery of one man's true identity.

This book has been written to persuade the reader that there is someone who believes in you, someone who wants to tell you that you are loved. As you read this story, discover the truth that can separate you from your past and set you on a course for a future without limits.

—Chris Schwab

THE BEGINNING OF MY LIFE

chapter one

Mom and Dad

MY PARENTS ARE MARGARET AND STEPHEN MCNEIL. MY MOM WAS twenty-six years old when she became pregnant with me. Dad was twenty-nine at the time. My oldest sister, Selena, was four years old when I was born, and my sister Jamie Lynn was two.

Selena was born a full month overdue. When Jamie Lynn was born, it was a very difficult birth for my mother. There were many complications during the pregnancy and Jamie was born almost two months premature. Shortly after my parents brought her home, her lungs began to collapse and they rushed her back to the hospital. Jamie actually stopped breathing and was resuscitated a couple of times while in emergency.

After Jamie Lynn's birth, Mom's doctor told her that she shouldn't become pregnant again. Mom had been in a serious motor vehicle accident and was told that another pregnancy could result in worse complications, and possibly paralysis. Both of my parents were heavy drinkers and used marijuana. They felt a great deal of fear when they learned that my mom was pregnant again. Very early in the pregnancy, Mom began to have problems which quickly developed into paralysis from the waist down. To save my mother's life, she and my father felt that abortion was their only option.

Mom went to her doctor and talked over the methods available to her: a surgical abortion or a chemical abortion. Because she was in the early stages of the pregnancy, my parents decided on a chemical abortion. A chemical abortion uses methotrexate and misoprostol. Methotrexate is given by injection and is intended to kill the fetus and terminate the pregnancy. It breaks down the cell layer that attaches the embryo to the walls of the uterus, depriving it of essential nutrients and resulting in the embryo's death. The misoprostol then causes the cervix to soften and dilate, and the uterus to contract and expel the embryo. Chemical abortions are used up to the seventh week of pregnancy.

This method required several visits to the doctor. During the first visit, Mom was told about the abortion options. In the second, she was given the methotrexate by injection. She was also given misoprostol tablets and was told to take them orally a couple of days after the injection. Mom was told this part of the process could be painful and accompanied by much bleeding.

Somewhere between the methotrexate injection and the misoprostol pills, she changed her mind about having another baby, deciding that she didn't want to terminate me. But she had already received the injection; if she didn't go through with the rest of the process, there would be serious complications. When a chemical abortion doesn't result in removal of the embryo, a surgical abortion must be performed.

All of these things must have caused a great deal of stress and anxiety. At my mother's next appointment, the doctor couldn't believe she hadn't taken the misoprostol. He immediately scheduled

> The news they received was very shocking: my mother was still pregnant and I was still very much alive.

tests to determine what the next step should be. The news they received was very shocking: my mother was still pregnant and I was still very much alive.

Birth

I was born Tanya Elizabeth McNeil on November 1, 1969, at the Henderson General Hospital in Hamilton, Ontario, Canada.

Boy or Girl

My earliest memories, from five or six years of age, are of a life filled with confusion. My mom and dad were raising me in the same way they had raised their other two daughters—but I didn't think or feel like a girl. All of the things I wanted to do were not girl things. When I was given dolls or toys that a girl would enjoy, I used them the way a boy would. Tearing the heads off the dolls seemed to be a favourite for me. I didn't want to be a girl; I wanted to be a boy.

Mom would buy me girl clothes, but I didn't want to wear girl clothes. When we would go out as a family to visit friends,

*Grade one picture from
my dad's wallet.*

my mom would tell us to wear dressy clothes. That was my cue to find one of my dad's western shirts and old cowboy boots. That was my idea of dress-up. After a few attempts, my mom began to make my sisters responsible for getting me ready. I would be forced to wear the girly clothes they thought I should wear. In my mind, all those frilly and puffy things weren't for me. I wanted to be a boy.

I clearly remember one incident that resulted in discipline from my dad. I had watched other boys do something I thought I should be able to do: I snuck out behind the garage, behind a small bush, and tried to pee standing up. That seemed to me much easier than always having to sit down. I was just beginning to realize that it wasn't working out the way I had imagined when I heard my father shout at me: "What in the world do you think you're doing? That is not the way girls do that!" I knew he was right because I could feel the evidence running down my legs.

I still wanted to be a boy.

Another incident from my early years brings shame every time I think about it. I forced a girl about the same age as me to strip. Then, after she was done, I bribed her not to tell anyone. I think I wanted to see if other girls were the same as I was.

I still wanted to be a boy.

I guess I was hoping that she would be different than me and I would have proof that I was actually a boy.

About fifteen years later, I met a young woman at an AA meeting and she asked if I remembered her. I told her I did not. She then proceeded to tell me that she was the girl I had forced to strip for me. I had no idea what to say. After some embarrassing moments, she seemed willing to let me off the hook. We joked about it and became friends for a while.

Assault

One day when I was seven years old, I stayed home with my dad and one of his friends. We were all sitting in the living room watching TV when Dad's friend asked me where the bathroom was.

"Up the stairs and the first door on the right," I told him.

"Would you show me the way, please?"

"I told you, up the stairs and the first door on the right."

I think I said it a little loud and a little rude because my dad spoke up. "Show the man where the bathroom is, Tanya!"

"Yes, Dad."

I led the man upstairs and was going to step out of the way for him to go into the bathroom at the top. He had other ideas. He pushed me into the bathroom and closed the door behind us. He then sexually molested me.

He told me that he would kill my mother if I told anyone what he had done.

> The man told me that he would kill my mother if I told anyone what he had done.

When I left the bathroom, I ran to my bedroom. I went to the corner of the room and sat alone for many hours. I refused to have a bath for almost a week and would not use the bathroom unless the door was open partway and someone in my family was standing outside talking to me. To this day, the door must be open a little bit when I use a washroom.

I Wanted Second Prize

I was eight years old when my family moved to an acreage on Ridge Road near Grimsby, Ontario. Some of the land was a vineyard, and we were renting the house and yard. Dad had bought a large quarter horse, Candy, which my sisters would ride up and down the rows of vines. I constantly bugged Mom and Dad to let me ride Candy through the vines, but they always said I was too young. Finally, after many attempts to persuade them, they relented and gave me permission to ride Candy by myself.

I didn't know at the time that my sisters had trained Candy to walk the full length of the vineyard and then gallop back on the return leg. As I rode Candy down the rows away from the house, I continually kicked her, trying to get her to go faster. I tried everything I could to get that horse to go faster, but she just kept walking along between the rows of grape vines.

As Candy started to make the turn at the end and begin to gallop, I furiously kicked her one more time. I think she was finally fed up with me because she broke into a flat-out gallop. Now I was screaming and hanging on for my life. Candy quickly left the vineyard and started around the back of the barn. Right in front of us was Dad's old Chevy. That didn't bother Candy at all, because she was a retired showjumper. Next thing I knew, we were flying. When we landed, I bounced out of the saddle and ended up standing in one stirrup holding on to the horn like a trick rider. I was just about back into the saddle when I heard Dad yell, "Candy, Stop!" Candy stopped almost instantly, but I did not. I continued forward onto Candy's head and almost took a header into the dirt. I looked down into Candy's eyes and could see she had enjoyed scaring the pants off me. I wasn't injured, but I think that was the last time I ever rode Candy.

On my eighth birthday, my dad brought home a little black pony. I immediately named her Blackie. Dad told me that Blackie was for all his children, but I always thought she was my birthday present. I had no problem riding Blackie safely. We spent many hours riding up and down the rows in the vineyard. We would tie Blackie to a tree in the middle of the front yard on a long leash and watch her graze for hours.

One afternoon as we watched Blackie graze, a man drove up and began to talk to us about Blackie. We talked for a little while about the horse and then he asked us if we would come to his church on Sundays for Sunday school. We had never been to church before, but our parents agreed. He told us he was having a contest with prizes for the kids who brought the most friends with them. He also told us he would pick us up every Sunday during the summer.

Each Sunday he would show up, and my sister Jamie and I would have a bunch of our friends waiting to go. Jamie and I loved

One of my favorite plaid shirts! A leather vest or a simple pair of suspenders made the perfect accessory!

to compete against one another. We would make a contest out of anything. I remember nothing about what they taught us at Sunday school, but I was sure I was going to win first place. We didn't know what the prizes were going to be, but I wanted first prize anyway.

Finally, at the end of summer, they announced the prize winners. My sister Jamie won second prize with six friends and I won first prize with seven friends. I was so excited. My prize was a new fish aquarium and a fish for every friend I had brought. Jamie's prize was a new white Bible.

I was so angry. I wanted the Bible. I had won the contest, but I wanted the second prize more than the first prize. I don't remember why I wanted the Bible more than the aquarium.

School Years

My school years weren't so much a time of learning as they were a battle zone. I failed grades two, four, and six. I was expelled from grade six the second time around because I was constantly fighting.

One of my recurring feelings was isolation. I felt like my family tried to keep me separated from other children my age. This may be partly because of my behaviour, and partly because

I felt picked on and ridiculed. In response to the isolation and ridicule, I got angry and become a bully. The feelings of isolation may also be a result of my family moving so much as I was growing up.

My problems in school were also related to a learning disability called dyslexia. I didn't have a problem with reversing letters, but whole words would seem to be missing as I read. I would need to slow down and read things three or four times before I could see and comprehend all the words.

Bluegrass

Music was a large part of my family's life. My dad played music professionally, and all of us sang with him at different times. Among my favourite summer outings was attending bluegrass festivals. If there was a festival within three or four hours' driving distance, we were there.

I remember the gospel bluegrass more vividly than any other kind. I would work my way right up to the stage when I knew the next group would be singing gospel. My all-time favourite was a song called "Heaven." It still brings a tear to my eye when I listen to it. It always reminds me of the good times we had as a family at those festivals. Bluegrass was, in some way, my introduction to God.

My dad would occasionally perform at the festival when they were short a musician. He loved to be a part of jam sessions around the nightly campfire. One weekend, he was scheduled to do a few songs but he had injured his right hand. He decided that he and I could do it together. He stood holding his guitar and fretting as he usually did while I stood behind him and strummed his guitar with my right hand. We didn't get it perfect, but everyone enjoyed the attempt.

Another reason I liked the bluegrass festivals was that they gave me an opportunity to earn some pocket money. The music and partying would go on until two or three in the morning, but I always fell asleep early. I would get up at four and go out with some of the other kids to round up beer bottles. By the time everyone else was up, I would have the back of our van loaded with empties. The rest of my family complained about the stale beer smell all the way home, but I didn't mind.

Pot

When I was growing up, my mom and dad, and some of their friends, were involved in growing marijuana. Some of their friends and family were corn farmers, so they did the growing. They would plant pot in small plots in the middle of the corn fields, and the corn would grow taller than the marijuana plants and hide them from view. At that time there were no police helicopters, so they had no fear of the pot being spotted from the air.

When harvest time came, they would all take turns bringing in the crop. The next step in the business was getting together at our house to package the pot for sale. My parents would never admit they were selling; they always claimed it was for "personal use." Most members of the group were regular users themselves, including my mom and dad.

Uncle Ralph was a member of the Hamilton Police Force, Narcotics Division. He wasn't really our uncle, but that's what everyone called him. One night, when the crowd was gathered at our house, Officer Ralph decided to come by and pay a visit to some of his friends. He approached the house, opened the door, and walked into the kitchen where everyone was busy dividing and packaging the pot. He immediately did an about-face, walked out the door, closed it behind him, and loudly knocked.

"Hamilton Police Force, Narcotics Division," he yelled.

"Just a minute," my father said.

The family quickly cleaned up any evidence of what they had been doing and let Uncle Ralph into the house. Of course he knew what was going on, but he never mentioned the family hobby. Everyone did their best to protect everyone else from any hint of wrongdoing.

I first experimented with pot when I was in my early teens, and Mom or Dad made sure I used the "good stuff." I guess they thought they were protecting me from picking up some bad stuff on the street. From then on, it became a regular part of my life, just as much as having a few drinks was a regular part of most parties.

Dad

As a musician, my dad spent most of his time playing in bars and clubs. I didn't see him much during my school years. If I came home from school and saw that the stereo was gone from the living room, I knew Dad had been caught cheating on Mom and she had kicked him out again. When Dad's nice stereo returned, we knew that he was back in favour with Mom.

One day I came home and saw Dad moving the stereo into his car. He gave me twenty dollars and told me to go to the store and buy myself something. I guess he was embarrassed, because twenty bucks was a lot of money then.

Over the years, I caught my dad cheating three times and ratted him out to my mom every time. I loved my dad, but I couldn't understand why he would cause my mother such pain.

White Lightning

When I was thirteen years old, I became friends with another girl who lived in the same apartment building as my family. One day, she brought out some pills and told my friend Gina and I that they were very strong vitamins. She had taken them from her mother's medicine cabinet. We divided them up between us and ended up taking six and a half pills each. The girl who gave them to us said we should run around, and that would activate the vitamins quicker.

My next memory was waking up in the living room of my sister's best friend's apartment. I was talking to a police officer who had two heads. Then my sister Jamie came into

> I was talking to a police officer who had two heads.

the room, and she had two heads as well. I realized my right wrist was extremely painful. Jamie told me I had run into the building where we lived like someone was chasing me, and then I'd fallen down the stairs near the entrance and broken my wrist.

Gina and I had spent almost four hours running around our neighbourhood and doing stuff we would never be able to remember. My family later learned from the police that the drugs the girl had taken from her mother were called White Lightning.

85-86 Hockey season

THE BEGINNING OF MY FAMILY

chapter two

Boot Camp

I GRADUATED FROM HIGH SCHOOL IN THE SUMMER OF 1988, AFTER THE usual four years and before my nineteenth birthday. Shortly after starting high school, I'd been tested and found to be capable of doing schoolwork beyond my age. They had tested me because I had finished the full year's math curriculum in six weeks. My problem was my inability to get along with the other students. I was two or three years older than my classmates, so they decided to promote me through grades seven and eight.

I had broken up with my boyfriend shortly after high school and felt like nobody wanted me. I decided to see if the military would take me, and they did. I signed up for basic training at CFB Cornwallis.

I soon realized that I was there for all the wrong reasons. After breaking up with my boyfriend, I just wanted to be somewhere else—not a good reason to join the navy. I soon began to miss my friends and family at home. I decided it was time to manipulate my way out of the military.

I called my mom and asked her to contact my superiors and tell them I was needed at home. I don't know if she did it or not, but that tactic got no results. The padre at the base received a number of visits from me as I tried to convince him I wasn't mentally fit, maybe even suicidal. Nothing worked. I wanted out but couldn't make it happen.

1989 Basic Training

Foot Locker

During a routine locker inspection, our platoon officer could inspect anything in our lockers except what was in our personal items box. That was off-limits to everyone. Well, I had made the mistake of leaving a small photo album out of the box, and during the inspection the officer looked through it. He began making rude comments about the people I loved. He told me that my parents were fat, my nephews were homely, and all my women friends were probably my lesbian lovers.

I was extremely lonely and didn't have any friends in basic training, so I was vulnerable to his insults. Seething inside, I asked him for permission to speak freely. When permission was given,

I proceeded to verbally abuse and insult him in return, not caring what the consequences might be.

After that, the officer began to inspect everything in my locker with a ruler. All of the measurements had to be exact. The underwear had to be folded to exactly four inches by four inches, the pants couldn't have railroad tracks pressed into them, and all the socks had to be smiling perfectly.

One day I was informed that I had failed the inspection, which warranted a complete locker shelf reboot. Every shelf was knocked down and I had to redo everything to the correct dimensions and put it all in perfect order.

I believed the whole process was intended to humiliate me. I felt that even the military rejected me, and I missed my family and friends even more.

Near the end of my basic training, I had a serious fall and tore up my knee. I was placed in suspended training and told that the military doctors wanted to operate to repair my knee. I requested a release instead and was granted an honourable discharge.

One-Night Stand

During my teenage years, confusion about my gender—and more specifically about sex—continued to haunt me. I always felt different than the boys and girls I grew up with. I felt attracted to the girls but knew society said that was wrong. I had even experimented with dating girls but always felt torn between my feelings and what I had been taught by my family. I had tried to be a "good girl" and only date boys, but that was less satisfying. I had a continual sense of being out of place whoever I was with. Being around married couples or dating singles who enjoyed being together was torment for me. I believed I would never be able to have that kind of happiness. I spent many hours considering and actively planning suicide. It seemed my only means of escape.

One evening I went to a bar with a group of people, including my best friend at the time. John and I had known each other for a couple of years. We had tried dating before I joined the military, but I was very uncomfortable with it. After I entered basic training, I wrote him a "Dear John" letter and told him I didn't want a romantic relationship with him. I knew I was a woman physically, but emotionally I was someone different. My relationship with him, I thought, was like a friendship between men.

That night, all of us became quite drunk and the conversation between John and I turned to sex. We began talking about my confusion regarding my sexuality. My physical sex and my emotional sex were all mixed up. I told him that I didn't know who or what I was. We talked about the fact

> *My physical sex and my emotional sex were all mixed up.*

that he had cerebral palsy and how that could affect his sex life. Both of us were very drunk and the conversation turned to the topic of sex with one another. Having drowned our inhibitions, we decided to give it a try. We found our way to my apartment on Cannon Street and had sex.

Rejected

I didn't talk to John again until about a month later when I found out I was pregnant. Now I was really in turmoil. Not only did I not want to be a woman, I was pregnant. I didn't want any part of the way my life was turning out.

I called John and asked if we could get together and talk. He didn't want to do that, but wouldn't tell me why. Later I found out he was dating someone else and wasn't interested in me any longer. He demanded I tell him what I wanted to talk about. I didn't want to tell him over the phone, but I finally blurted out that I was pregnant. After a long pause, I received a very cold response: "As far as I'm concerned, get rid of it." I didn't hear from him again until two or three years later.

> I didn't even want to be a woman, but here I was having one of the most important experiences of a woman's life.

The realization that I had given myself to a man who had no interest in me beyond a one-night stand was extremely humiliating. I had surrendered something that should have been precious to me. I felt used and unwanted, but I also realized I was responsible for where my life was headed. I wanted to hate John, and I wanted to hate myself. I wanted to get rid of the baby, thinking that would somehow punish John for what he had done.

I didn't even want to be a woman, but here I was having one of the most important experiences of a woman's life. I knew I would need to make a decision soon about the future of my child. I also knew that whatever my decision was, I would be making this journey on my own.

My first step was to go to my doctor and talk about my options. He knew I had been taking medications, including narcotics, as a result of a motor vehicle accident a couple of months prior. He did some tests and discovered I was carrying a healthy baby. I told the doctor that my baby was a fighter; I would not kill him and I determined to fight for life along with him.

Reliving the Assault

The following summer, I was with my family at an event at a local park. We were all enjoying an evening of music and dancing. While dancing with one of my nephews, I noticed an older man dancing with a young girl. My memories immediately flashed back to the sexual assault when I was seven years old. This was the man who had lured me into the bathroom and abused me.

I felt I was reliving that horrible experience. My older sister Selena noticed that I was hyperventilating and in distress, and she rushed over to ask what was wrong. I pointed out the man. She recognized him, told me his name, and wanted to know why seeing him had produced such a reaction. I proceeded to tell her that fourteen years earlier, that man had molested me in the bathroom.

Selena found the story difficult to believe. She had spent a lot of time with the man and his family when she'd been younger. She assured me that he had never done anything inappropriate to her. It took some time, but I eventually persuaded her that I was telling the truth. Selena then comforted me and we decided to leave the park.

Later that day, I related my experience to my parents, telling them that he had assaulted me many years before in the upstairs bathroom. The sight of the man had caused some deep emotions to resurface. I felt as if I was reliving that terrible experience over and over again in my thoughts and emotions.

My mother's reaction was to have me seek counselling. My father wanted to hunt the man down and kill him. He was angry and hurt that someone could do that to his child in their own home. Mom and I had a difficult time convincing him not to do that. I had been victimized by this man, but I didn't want my father doing anything to land himself in jail. We finally agreed that the best option was to forget the past and go forward.

Being pregnant at the time escalated my emotional difficulties. The next year, I did go for counselling through a program for adult survivors of childhood sexual abuse. They mentioned the possibility of filing charges, but I decided against it. I had lived through the abuse once and was unwilling to do it again in a public forum.

Divorced

My mom and dad did not have a close relationship. Early in their marriage, as I mentioned, Dad had begun running around on my mother. She would put up with it for a short time but then end up kicking him out of the house. A few weeks later, Dad would find a way to talk Mom into taking him back and he would move home again.

After this cycle had repeated itself a number of times, Mom finally filed for divorce in January 1990. The divorce was finalized on February 13, 1991.

My Son Jesse

Jesse Lee Daniel McNeil was born at Joseph Brant Memorial Hospital in Burlington, Ontario on August 24, 1990. I brought him home to my apartment on Main Street in Hamilton.

Jesse was my responsibility and I wanted to keep him safe. He was dependant on me for everything a young, growing child needs, but loving and caring for him as a mother didn't seem natural to me. I had watched my mother and sisters care for their children, so in many ways I felt like I was faking it. I knew I was Jesse's mother, but in my heart I wanted to be his dad. I knew I could be good at that.

At two months of age, Jesse began to get sick frequently. At six months, he was diagnosed as having asthma and pneumonia. After a short stay in the hospital, he came home with a medical nebulizer to help control the asthma. I realized the cold, roach-infested place we were living in was harmful to my son, so we moved.

> I knew I was Jesse's mother, but in my heart I wanted to be his dad.

Jesse continued to have health problems through his early years. He was on Ventolin, through a nebulizer, until he was seven years old. He was also hospitalized with roseola before his first birthday. By age five, he had his tonsils and adenoids removed, and tubes put in his ears due to chronic tonsillitis and ear infections.

At one point I called my mother and asked her to come and rescue Jesse. I was beginning to think about harming him in some way. My life and my family seemed totally out of control.

Paternity

Jesse was one year old when I contacted John again and asked him to help us. We were living on welfare at the time and the government's policy was that the father should pay child support. Welfare forced me to call John and ask him to voluntarily pay support. He refused, because he denied he was the father.

Jesse Lee Daniel McNeil

Before Jesse was conceived, I had been sharing an apartment with another man. John knew about this and said that the other man was Jesse's father. I knew this wasn't true, because we had only ever shared the apartment; we were never involved in a sexual relationship. John was the only man I had ever had sex with.

Welfare referred me to a lawyer who arranged for the paternity test. John went to have a blood test, followed by Jesse and I having the same test. The results showed that John was the father to a 99.99% certainty.

The next step was to go before a judge and receive a judgment against John. The judge said that John had shown no interest in Jesse so he was not given any visitation rights. He was also ordered to pay seventy-five dollars per month until Jesse turned nineteen. I received that money every month for the next eighteen years, until Jesse's nineteenth birthday.

Tonia

After living at home for a few months, I got another job and decided it was time for Jesse and me to be on our own again. We got a large apartment and I decided to rent out a room to help with the expenses. Tonia, a friend of mine, and her young daughter Kayla moved in. Jesse and Kayla each had their own room while Tonia and I slept in separate beds in the master bedroom. Tonia had recently broken up with her boyfriend, Kayla's father.

I soon realized that I was going to have problems with the sleeping arrangements. I found out I was attracted to Tonia. Tonia and I weren't involved in any physical relationship, but I began to spend a lot of time imagining what it would be like. I was again face to face with a crisis of identity; I had

> *I was thinking like a man trapped in a woman's body.*

been raised to believe that two women having a sexual relationship was wrong. I thought about it a lot—but I thought about it as if I was the man in the relationship. Again I was thinking like a man trapped in a woman's body.

Tonia and I began to get involved in marijuana and other drugs. We both had friends who used pot on a regular basis, so it was easy for us to join them in regular use and experimenting with new ways to use pot.

After a couple of months, Tonia asked if her former boyfriend could move in with us. I should have said no, but instead I reluctantly agreed. He had been verbally and physically abusive before they split up, but he assured her that he was a changed man. It didn't take too long before he was again yelling and insulting Tonia and Kayla. That was hard enough to endure, but one day I heard him yell and curse at my son. I couldn't allow that to continue.

I called my sisters—and their large, strong husbands—and asked them to help me get these people out of my home. When Tonia and her boyfriend came home the next day, we were all waiting for them and had their stuff packed. Thankfully, they agreed to leave peacefully.

Intervention

I was involved in a motor vehicle accident in December 1989. As a result, I had begun taking several medications, including some narcotics. My doctor had stopped all my medications while I was pregnant with Jesse, but after he was born I convinced the doctor that I needed them again.

I made appointments with other doctors, and after an examination and discussion they were convinced I had postpartum depression and they gave me more prescriptions. I soon realized I had found an easy way to get all the drugs and medications I wanted. Over the next couple of years, I became an expert at convincing doctors of my need for an ever-growing list of prescription drugs.

One day, Jesse and I went to my mom's place for a visit. Jesse enjoyed visiting his grandma. As we were preparing to leave, one of the bags I had with me tipped over and eighteen to twenty pill bottles fell out and spilled their contents onto the floor. I scrambled to gather them up and put everything back in the bag, but Mom came into the room and saw what I was doing.

She had a horrified look on her face and asked me what I was doing with all of those pills. In embarrassment and anger, I told her it was none of her business. After I left, I was ashamed of how rude I had been to my mother and regretted speaking to her that way. I realized how out-of-control my life had become.

A few days later, Jamie invited me to her house for supper. When I walked in, I saw that my whole family was there. I quickly realized they had planned an intervention on me.

My mother related to them what she had seen when I had spilled all my medications on her floor. All of them began expressing their concerns and fears for my life, and for Jesse.

I became very defensive and angry. What I did with my life was my responsibility, not theirs. I reminded them of their drinking and pot-smoking ways. As far as I could see, they were all hypocrites. Soon we were all shouting insults at one another.

My sister quietly walked over to me, took my face between her hands, and looked me in the eyes. "I don't want you to die!"

I broke down and began to cry uncontrollably. My family's concerns for my life finally got through to me. This wasn't about my family trying to control my life; this was about their desire to save my life. They were expressing their love for me and trying to convince me to seek help. I knew I needed help, but I didn't know how or where to get it.

Selena told me they had made arrangements with a hospital to have me admitted. They had convinced the doctors that I was suicidal, and I would not be released until the doctors were convinced I no longer wanted to end my life. My mother said she would take care of Jesse while I was in the hospital, and I could live with her after I was through withdrawal. I agreed to go through the program they had arranged.

> This wasn't about my family trying to control my life; this was about their desire to save my life.

I had no idea what I had agreed to. The first couple of days of withdrawal weren't too difficult. For the next couple of days, I was physically ill with extended bouts of vomiting. Then the real pressures and pain of my drug habits set in. I didn't realize how much I needed the medications to help me cope with my life. They were the only way I could supress my mental torment. I suddenly was face-to-face with my identity crisis. I didn't know who I was, and without the drugs I again wanted to end my existence. The medications had provided a way for me to not think about who I was. As my thinking became clearer, the only way I could mask the pain was to become angry.

I had spent a large part of my childhood in a state of battle. I'd fought with my parents and teachers, constantly getting into fistfights with my classmates and "friends." I hadn't been able to keep friends for long because I beat them away. When I thought about my life, I would end up thinking, *Who am I? Why do I look like a woman when I know I am a man?*

I began to express my anger towards anyone and everyone around me. I argued with the staff. I complained about the food. I disobeyed the rules and yelled at the nurses. I got into physical fights with other patients. I did anything I could to prevent being quiet and having to think about who or what I really was.

While in rehab, I was told by my family that they couldn't recover any of the large possessions from the apartment I'd been living in. The landlord had re-rented the apartment and they were given a limited amount of time to retrieve my stuff. In the end, they were able to remove some of the small things, but none of the furniture. When I finally got out of rehab, I would definitely have to start all over again. Of course, this didn't help my anger.

> *Who am I? Why do I look like a woman when I know I am a man?*

There weren't many things to do between doctors' visits and group discussions. In one of the common rooms, the hospital had shelves packed with games and jigsaw puzzles. I began to spend much of my time doing puzzles. They became a way to focus on something other than myself. I didn't want to think about my life.

Another effect of withdrawal was feeling as though my skin was crawling. I was always looking for a way to scratch and relieve that feeling. One day, trying to relieve that crawling feeling, I rubbed my body all over the inside of a phone booth. A nurse caught me and made me go to my room for a couple of hours as punishment. I felt very antisocial at the time, so it wasn't much of a punishment.

The staff wouldn't give me any indication as to when I would be allowed to go home.

> *I had no real desire for change; I just wanted out.*

After a couple of weeks of being uncooperative, I was told by the doctors that my defiance was preventing my release. I very quickly developed some good behaviour to show them I was going to follow the rules and earn my release. I had no real desire for change; I just wanted out.

After a couple more weeks, I convinced them I was free from suicidal tendencies, and they sent me home.

One Last Attempt

When Jesse was four or five years old, he began asking me why he didn't have a dad. I decided to contact John again. John was married by this time, so I asked if they would both like to meet Jesse. I met John by myself first. Our meeting went well, so we decided on a time for John and his wife to come to my place and visit Jesse.

When they arrived at the house, Jesse ran upstairs to his room and refused to come down. Later John went upstairs to talk to Jesse for a few minutes, but when he came down he told his wife they were leaving. John never responded to any of my or Jesse's phone calls from that point on.

THE BEGINNING OF MY SEARCH

chapter three

Barbara

WHEN I WAS TWENTY-SIX YEARS OLD, I CONVINCED MY FRIEND Michelle to come with me to check out some of the gay bars in Hamilton. I was continuing to look for my identity, but the predominant feeling was that I was a man trapped in a woman's body. I knew I was physically a woman; I had given birth to a son who was now six years old. I was also very aware that I was physically attracted to other women. I thought I was attracted to women as a man would be, not as a woman. There seemed to be a continual conflict inside me.

Michelle and I started to make the rounds of the gay bars and clubs. Every couple of weeks we would go to a dance club, the drag bar, or the karaoke bar. All of these places catered to the gay and lesbian community.

One night, I met a woman named Barbara at one of the bars. We began watching the shows together, having a few drinks and talking. She told me she was living a lesbian lifestyle and was interested in me as a partner. I didn't know who I was at the time, but I knew I was very attracted to her. I thought I would need to try that type of relationship if I was to discover who I was.

Barbara moved into my place and I began to explore what a lesbian relationship was like. We quickly discovered that we both wanted to be the "man" in our family. Things did not go well. After about a year, I decided to kick Barbara out. I wasn't at home when she came to get her things, but a friend of mine, Charlene, was there with Jesse.

> She told me she was living a lesbian lifestyle and was interested in me as a partner.

Barbara picked up her stuff, stole my set of drums, and even tried to take Jesse. Barbara told Charlene that because she had lived with me for a year, Jesse was her son, too. Thankfully, Charlene wouldn't allow Barbara to take him with her. It's possible I may never have seen him again.

Brooke

I decided that I really needed to stay single for a while. My physical relationships had all proved disastrous, but I wanted to continue going to gay clubs. I enjoyed the drag shows and participated in karaoke regularly. One of the biggest attractions for me was the music, being raised around clubs and bars with my dad. Performing had been a large part of my life growing up.

One night at the karaoke bar, while hanging around the pool table and enjoying the show, I began to dance and sing along with the performers. I got lost in the music and didn't notice what was going on around me. Suddenly, one of my friends got my attention and told me that most of the customers were watching my performance instead of the one on stage. Not only was my performance noticed by the other customers, I had come to the attention of Tracy, the Queen Mom at the club.

When the set was finished, Tracy went up to the microphone and asked me to join her on stage. I thought she was preparing to throw me out of the club, but she told me later that she had intended to humiliate me instead. She decided to issue a challenge: I could do four songs the following week, on stage; I would have to do the first two songs as a woman and the second set as a man. I think I surprised her by accepting the challenge.

> Being a "female imperson-ator" felt all wrong, but this felt right.

Tracy assigned a drag queen named Jane to help me out with makeup and clothes for the first set as a woman. The songs I chose were ones I'd used to sing with my dad.

After I finished the first set, I rushed home, showered to get rid of the "woman" makeup, and went back to the club to get into the "man" makeup and clothing. With my hair slicked back and the western wear on, I felt like a man. Being a "female imperson-ator" felt all wrong, but this felt right. I decided to do two of my favourite songs by Garth Brooks.

When I finished the show, and noticed all the attention and applause I was getting, I realized I was hooked. I had found something I could do well and enjoy. Tracy had meant the challenge as a way to put me down, but she could see how much I enjoyed being a male impersonator and asked if I would like to do a regular show. I said yes immediately. Tracy asked me what she should use as my stage name, and "Brooke" was the first thing to pop into my mind.

A Star Is Born

Very soon I was doing shows almost every weekend. Many men performed as female impersonators, but I was one of only a few females performing as a man.

The drag scene in Hamilton became a big part of my life. I became closer to the other performers than I was to my own family. Because we were putting on shows in nightclubs and bars, everything we did included alcohol and drugs on a regular basis. I knew my life was headed in a direction that would soon get beyond my control.

On my mother's birthday, I decided to surprise her with some flowers. She knew about my performances but had never seen a show. I bought her a nice bouquet and got dressed for the show that night. I stopped by Mom's place on my way to the club. When she opened the door, I knew from her expression that she didn't recognize me.

We talked for a few minutes about my show, and as I was leaving she gave me a kiss and said I looked great, but the stuff I had on my lips tasted gross.

My son Jesse was six years old when I was involved in the drag scene, and I sometimes left him at home by himself. One evening while I was getting dressed and putting on my makeup, Jesse walked into my room, looked at me in the mirror, and asked if he could call me Dad.

I realized that my son was becoming as confused as I was. I was living as much like a man as I could. I believed that I should have been born a boy. I felt as if my whole world was backwards, but the time I spent as a male impersonator didn't feel like I was pretending to be someone else. I began believing that "Brooke" was the real me.

Every year, the gay community in Hamilton held a competition called the Skyway Pageant. Performers had to make an application, perform their show for the judges, and then be interviewed. They then elect a Mr. Skyway from the male impersonators, a Miss Skyway from the female impersonators, and a Mr. and Miss Gay Hamilton from the gay men and women. All of the winners were announced at the end of the pageant.

> I began believing that "Brooke" was the real me.

The very first year I entered, I won the Mr. Skyway crown. Part of the responsibilities after winning was providing hospitality for the annual coronation ball. I was expected to be part of all of our events because Mr. and Miss Skyway were the face of the gay community in Hamilton. I really enjoyed doing the shows as Brooke, but this persona was slowly taking over my life.

After every show, I would go home and slowly remove the costume and makeup. It felt like I was removing the real me. I wanted to stop pretending to be a man part of the time and live like a man all the time.

Moving

The club scene in Hamilton gave me the opportunity to meet and date many different women. One of them was Allison, who came to see one of my shows. I met Allison after my set and was eventually encouraged to ask her on a date. We began spending lots of time together and often stayed up all night talking. After a couple of months, Allison asked me to move into her apartment with her.

Shortly after I moved in with Allison, a rainstorm caused a flood in her apartment and we had to be evacuated. I moved back home with my mom, and Allison stayed with some friends for a couple of weeks.

After we found out that the apartment was going to be unliveable for another six months, we decided to move together to a small town in southern Ontario. I got a job working as a flagger on road construction jobs.

The end of the work season came near the end of September, and we didn't have any work plans beyond the end of the season. That same week, our landlord gave us notice on the house we were renting. He needed the house for some of his relatives. We had to make a quick decision about what to do.

I told Allison that I'd always dreamed about moving out west. I related to her one of my earliest memories as a child, of getting into my dad's cowboy boots, which came up to my hips, and walking around the house pretending to be a cowboy. My dad performed mostly country music, so he had to look the part. After much discussion, Allison agreed and said, "Let's go!"

We had no idea what we were doing. We had very little money, no vehicle, and no plan. The first thing I did was buy an old van for five hundred dollars. Then I got a ten-day moving permit. I thought for sure that would be enough time to get to Calgary, our final destination. I borrowed my mom's vehicle insurance card, thinking that would somehow get us through if we were pulled over for some reason.

Allison had four children, and I had Jesse, who was nine years old. Allison's children were Melissa (thirteen), Adam (twelve), Albert (ten), and Mailyn (eight). We gave all the children backpacks and told them to pack one change of clothes, one set of pyjamas, and whatever else they wanted. We put everything else we owned into a moving company's truck. It would go into storage in Calgary until we arrived.

The plan was to take our time going across Canada and make it an educational trip for the kids. We did take our time. We had a great trip until we got near the Ontario/Manitoba border. The ten-day moving permit on the van was about to expire and we were leaving the province. We stopped in the last town before the border and went to a registry office to get another permit. I was told they weren't allowed to give a second moving permit immediately after a first permit, and I didn't have proper insurance. It looked like we were going to end our cross-Canada trip about halfway, but someone took pity on us. We left the office with another ten-day permit.

We resumed our sightseeing tour through Manitoba until we were pulled over by the RCMP in Saskatchewan. The officer had noticed our vehicle didn't have any licence plates. After I showed him the moving permit, he radioed his station because he wasn't familiar with that type of form. His co-workers had a good laugh at his expense and called him a rookie for not knowing about the moving permit. I guess he was embarrassed, because he let us continue without any ticket at all. He could have impounded the van right there, because he'd also noticed that I had an insurance card in someone else's name. He let us off with a stern warning and told us to get to Calgary before the permit expired. It's a good thing he didn't notice that it was our second permit. He probably would have thrown the book at us.

The holiday time was over, and now we had to hustle. We finally reached Calgary late at night with very little gas, and absolutely no money left for food or accommodations. We stopped at a phone booth and looked through the Yellow Pages for an organization that could help us. One of our first calls was to "Inn from the Cold," who immediately helped us with a week's lodging at a motel and vouchers for enough groceries to get us through the week. Another organization gave us five hundred dollars to pay the deposit on a small apartment. The St. Vincent De Paul Society gave us all new bedding. Allison contacted a friend, Mary, whom she'd met online, and Mary brought us a small television. Mary also contacted other friends, who gave us furniture. All of our possessions were in storage in Calgary, but we needed to get jobs and work for six months before we had the money to get them released.

The generosity of the people in Calgary was overwhelming. I look back now and realize that most of the money and gifts came from Christians. I'm very thankful for everything we received. I believe that's one of the reasons why Calgary feels so much like home to me.

THE BEGINNING OF MY CHANGE

chapter four

Change

NEAR THE END OF 1999, I WATCHED A DOCUMENTARY ABOUT FEMALE-to-male transsexuals. The program, called "The Invisible Transsexual" was about doctors and clinics in Montreal that helped people through the process of gender reassignment. Up until then, I didn't know about this possibility. I believed I was destined to live my life without any hope of real happiness. After the documentary was over, I went into my bedroom, curled up in the corner on the floor, and cried for hours, releasing all the fear and frustration that had built up in my life. That's where Allison found me hours later. She asked me what was wrong. I told her that the program we had just watched was my story—and I had to see my doctor.

I went to my doctor in Calgary and began discussions with him about my desire to pursue gender reassignment. I knew there were some steps I needed to go through before I could even think about the surgeries to physically become a man. The first was a "real-life test." I would be required to live as a man for a full year as an indication that I was serious about my desired gender. This would assist me in getting a referral to a doctor who would prescribe the surgeries. It would also help begin the process of finding a psychologist and endocrinologist to begin the hormone therapy.

After much discussion, my family doctor came to the conclusion that I had been attempting to live as a man for much of the past six years. I had been performing in drag clubs and dressing as a man. I was doing everything I could to be a man. I succeeded in persuading him that I had already passed the "real-life test." He referred me to the gender clinic in Calgary.

> *I was doing everything I could to be a man.*

The gender psychiatrist at the clinic instructed me to gather all the information I could find about gender reassignment. I began to search for anything available about the legal and physical processes necessary for the transition. I built a stack of paper at least three inches high of everything I found in libraries, online, and talking to people about gender reassignment.

Another important step was to get a legal name change. I had to make an appointment with the Calgary Police Service to get fingerprinted. Then I went to Alberta Registries to make an application. I took along the fingerprint document and my original birth certificate.

After I received my legal name change certificate, I updated my birth certificate, social insurance number, driver's licence, and Alberta health care card. I was now officially Travis Earl Stephen James McNeil.

The one change I couldn't get on my identification at this time was the "F" to "M" marker. To get the "female" changed to "male," I would have to wait until I had a letter from my surgeon saying that the gender reassignment surgeries had been completed.

I began the hormone treatments in 2000, when I was thirty-one years old. My family doctor oversaw my treatment because he had a special interest in gender reassignment.

The biggest hormonal change was taking testosterone, and as a result my voice got deeper, I began to develop body and facial hair, and I had an increased libido. Generally, I was in favour of all these changes. Occasionally while talking I would think I was hearing someone else.

Surgeries

My feelings about surgery were mixed. I'm not a big fan of physical discomfort, but I knew this was the next step in the process. Over the course of three surgeries at a Calgary hospital over three years, my breasts were removed. The surgeon botched the first operation, leaving me with large scars, which had to be corrected later. I also underwent a hysterectomy.

Though I did a considerable amount of research before all of my surgeries, I realize that I should have had more discussions with the surgeons. Perhaps additional consultations could have prevented some of the complications I experienced.

Moving Again

Throughout this process, Allison was a strong support for me. She understood my struggles and pain. She was familiar with all the physical and emotional issues associated with gender reassignment, having worked at a gender clinic in British Columbia when she was younger. The years we lived together weren't always turmoil-free, but I know that having her and her children around helped Jesse and I through many hard times. We really did feel like a family.

Allison and I began looking for a home to buy. We didn't have a down payment and knew we'd have a difficult time qualifying for a mortgage, so we looked into rent-to-own options. We found someone who had a house he would sell us using rent-to-own. We agreed to pay a higher rent than normal, but half the rent was to be kept towards the down payment for two years.

When the two years were up, we went to the mortgage company that the owner of the house had used. We were shocked to learn he hadn't been paying his mortgage on the house and the banks were foreclosing the property. Not only were we unable to purchase the house, but the foreclosure forced us to move out. We were also going to lose the extra money we had paid in rent. I could have recovered that money from the owner, but we couldn't afford the legal costs.

A real estate agent we knew heard about the situation and said he could help us get a mortgage for a house in a small town, much cheaper than in a city like Calgary. Allison found a house online in La Glace, Alberta, near Grande Prairie. We decided to pack up and move again.

I was working for a security company in Calgary at the time and my experience there helped me get a job in Grande Prairie. There was a high turnover rate in the security industry, so it was quite easy to get another job. This was important because I needed to quit my job before I went for my next surgery. The recovery time would be too long to just take holiday time, and I didn't want to explain to my employers and coworkers why I was gone from work for so long; changing jobs was my way out. Before each surgery, I would give my notice at work. Then, after my recovery, I would get a new job at another security company.

More Surgeries

I needed to travel to Montreal for my next operation, beginning the transformation of my female organs to male ones. The medical term for this is metoidioplasty. The surgeons also performed a scrotoplasty. Combined, these procedures took about four hours. The recovery time was three and a half weeks.

Back to Calgary

When I returned home from Montreal, I quickly noticed a change in my relationship with Allison. She was very cold and refused to be around me. I soon found out she was being unfaithful to me. I knew that what I was doing with my life would be hard for someone else to understand, but I had thought she would continue to be a support, as she had been before.

I packed up a few of my things and got on the bus back to Calgary.

I had mixed feelings about moving. Jesse was still in school, and I didn't want to take him out before the end of the school year. I was also concerned about how Allison and her children would treat him. Allison assured me that Jesse would be okay with them until school was out for the summer.

Before moving from Calgary to Grande Prairie, I had worked with a couple named Ervin and Byre. They had become close friends. Ervin and I had met back in February 2000, when I was just beginning hormone treatments, and he knew I was going through gender reassignment. One of his favourite comments during our early years working together was telling me, "You make a very ugly woman!"

> "You make a very ugly woman!"

He and Byre told me I could live with them for a while. I was now on employment insurance for three months and couldn't afford a place of my own. They were a great help to me. They were also willing to listen as I talked through my life struggles.

Jesse

Soon after settling in Calgary, I began to get emails from Jesse asking me when I was coming back to get him. I desperately wanted to go back to Grande Prairie to get my son, but the school year wasn't finished and I had no money to make the trip.

Then I got a phone call that changed everything. The principal of Jesse's school called me and said I should get Jesse out of Grande Prairie as soon as possible. He informed me that soon after I'd left, Jesse had started seeing the school councillor—and he'd told the councillor that he was made to feel like Cinderella at home. All the chores seemed to be his and Allison was verbally abusive. Allison was intercepting my emails to him, so he thought I didn't care about him, a feeling being reinforced by Allison and her children. The principal said he would pass Jesse in all of his subjects if I would agree to get him out of Grande Prairie right away.

When I told Ervin and Byre about the call, they knew I didn't have the money to go get Jesse, but they told me they would give me what I needed. They also decided to go with me to Grande Prairie.

When we got there, I wasn't prepared for the situation I found. Jesse was very happy to see me, but Allison wouldn't allow me to talk to her children. Even though we had lived together for seven years, and I had been a part of their lives, I was now completely cut off from them.

> *Even though we had lived together for seven years, and I had been a part of their lives, I was now completely cut off from Allison and her children.*

I wasn't permitted to enter the house and retrieve Jesse's clothing and the rest of my possessions. Allison gave us a garbage bag containing what she claimed were Jesse's clothes and eight boxes that were said to contain my possessions. We took the boxes to the bus depot and shipped them to Calgary because there wasn't enough room in the car. When we returned to Calgary, we found that the bag supposedly containing Jesse's clothes was actually old hand-me-downs and things that were already worn-out. I had to work at buying him a new set of clothing. The boxes containing my possessions were in worse shape; they were full of junk. The few things I recognized as mine were damaged beyond repair.

I felt completely cut off from the last seven years of my life. I didn't understand why this had happened, or what I had done to cause such a reaction. In some sense, I understood Allison ending our relationship for another man, but it seemed like everything she'd done to me and Jesse after our breakup had been intended to hurt us as much as possible. My emotions were in turmoil already because of the hormone treatments and surgeries.

I felt like a failure in my attempt at a family relationship.

Melissa

A couple of months after the move to Calgary, Allison's oldest daughter Melissa also moved to Calgary. Ervin and Byra didn't have an extra room, but Melissa moved in and slept on the couch. She and I talked about me leaving Grande Prairie, and how her mother had treated Jesse and me. Melissa had wanted to see me before we left, but Allison wouldn't allow it. Melissa was hurt by this and said I hadn't deserved to be treated that way. I was very happy to reconnect with Melissa, and I'm proud of her. Nine years later, I had the pleasure of standing in for her father and walking her down the aisle at her wedding.

One thing Melissa continually told me was that I needed to move forward with my life. She said that I should have a woman in my life again. I realized she was right, but I wasn't sure how to go about it. Melissa was prepared for that and told me about an online dating site. I had never thought about doing something like that, but I decided to give it a try. Melissa helped me set up an account, and I entered a search with some of my likes and dislikes. Two names came up. After sending an email to both of them, I waited for a response.

THE BEGINNING OF MY MARRIAGE

chapter five

First Date

I RECEIVED ONE EMAIL REPLY. TAMMY HATED EVERYTHING I HAD entered as my likes, so I have no idea why she even responded to me. We emailed back and forth for a few weeks and talked about the things I loved and she hated, and the things she loved and I hated. We discovered that there was very little we agreed on, but we continued to email one another.

Over the summer, we made plans to meet a couple of times, but it didn't happen. The first time we planned to meet, I got a call from another woman. I cancelled the date with Tammy. The second date we planned was a night out at a famous Calgary restaurant and bar. This time, Tammy stood me up.

Just before Tammy's thirty-ninth birthday on September 14, I got an email from her oldest daughter, Carrissa. She told me about Tammy's birthday and suggested that it would be a good time to get together with her. One night, a couple of days before Tammy's birthday and while emailing back and forth with small talk, I told her that I was eating my favourite dessert: pumpkin pie and ice cream.

"Where is my piece?" Tammy replied.

"In my fridge. Would you like some?"

"YES!"

"We will have to meet for that to happen."

"OK."

When Tammy and I met face to face for the first time, I was blown away by her looks. Her picture from the online dating service was very plain compared to the in-person Tammy. As I still tell anyone who will listen, I was captivated by her smokin' blue eyes.

As I walked up to meet her, I recognized her because she was surrounded by kids. We had talked about her children a lot online, so I was able to greet them all by name.

I had brought along Tammy's piece of pumpkin pie and a small bag of candies for her kids to share. We sat down and made the sort of small talk that goes with getting to know each other. Tammy's son Dustin told me that he really liked the Toronto Blue Jays jacket I was wearing. I let him wear it while Tammy and I talked.

We talked about children for a while, and somehow the conversation ended up on Wrestlemania 2006. We had discovered, during our conversations online, that we were both huge wrestling fans, and Wrestlemania 2006 was on television that night. We laughed about the fact that the dating site had matched us even though we had nothing in common in our profiles except wrestling.

I had no idea what to say or do when it was time to end our visit. Thankfully, Tammy's youngest daughter Angie solved the problem. She came over and gave me a big hug. So we had hugs all around and said goodbye. To this day, that is our family's way of greeting each other and saying goodbye.

Tammy and I had come to know each other quite well online, but now that I had actually met her, I wanted to be around her all the time. We began to meet regularly, even if it was just to go to 7-Eleven for a slurpee. Sometimes I would even need to borrow the money from Ervin, because I could never say no.

Ervin and Byra

Practically every time I came home after getting together with Tammy, Ervin would meet me at the door and ask, "Have you told her yet?" Of course, he was referring to me being a transsexual. "Not yet" was always my answer.

I was torn between wanting to do what was right and being afraid that telling her would be the end of our relationship. I think Ervin and Byra wanted me to reveal my past to Tammy because they were afraid I would get too close to her and then be hurt by her rejecting me when I did tell her. The closer I got to Tammy, the more I knew telling her was the right thing to do—but the closer I got, the more I feared a negative result.

> The closer I got to Tammy, the more I knew telling her was the right thing to do—but the closer I got, the more I feared a negative result.

They suggested we plan a double date, and that I tell Tammy then. We decided to go out for drinks and karaoke. Tammy agreed, so we set the date for November 4. When we got together that evening, everything was going well, but I became more nervous the later it got. I couldn't seem to find a time that felt right to bring up the subject. Ervin continued to give me signals to tell Tammy.

Byra finally asked to talk to me privately. She told me that I shouldn't tell Tammy that evening, but to wait and do it when we were alone together. I agreed, and we went back to our table. Tammy asked me if there was something I wanted to tell her. Under pressure, I said that I really liked her and wanted her to consider "going steady" with me. She said yes, and I was so relieved that I got totally plastered.

Now I had to tell Tammy I was a transsexual, and I had to apologize for being an idiot and getting drunk.

Tammy

The next morning, I went to Tammy's home determined to relate to her as much of my life as she wanted to hear. First, I said I was sorry for being drunk the night before and making a fool of myself.

A little later, we went into another room to have a cigarette. We always smoked away from her kids. We were alone, so I knew this was the opportunity. I needed to tell her who I was and what was going on in my life. I also knew I may be ending a relationship with someone I had come to care about very much.

I began by asking her why she had never asked me about Jesse's mother. She said that she didn't care about who she was. I then told her that I was Jesse's mother.

Tammy didn't seem to understand, so I started at my birth as Tanya Elizabeth McNeil and related my history, including my feelings growing up, to the start of hormone therapies and surgeries. I tried to squeeze as much of my life as possible into a short period of time.

> I also knew I may be ending a relationship with someone I had come to care about very much.

"Before you say anything. I'll understand if you want to break up, and I promise not to have any hard feelings." When I finally ran out of things to say, I asked, "Do you have any questions?"

Tammy was silent for a long period of time. "It doesn't matter," she finally said. "I enjoy being around the person you are now, not the person you used to be."

Then she leaned over and kissed me.

I pulled back. "You still want to kiss me?"

I was surprised because I had experienced so much rejection in my life, and I had prepared myself to be rejected again. If I hadn't known it before, I knew then: this was the woman I wanted to spend the rest of my life with.

Moved In

We spent all of our spare time together and I spent less and less time at Ervin and Byra's place, even though that was actually my home. I think Ervin and Byra were getting a little jealous because

I was never with them anymore. Tammy and I had talked about me moving in with her and her kids, but I didn't know if I wanted to do that.

Then something happened to make the decision easier.

A friend of mine had borrowed my debit card to get some money to pay a bill. I'm not sure why, but he completely drained my bank account. I couldn't believe a friend would do that, but now I was in a real bind. When I told Tammy about it, she said, "You need to move in with me and the kids."

Tammy already knew I had no money and that she would be supporting me until I was able to get a couple of paycheques at work. She was willing to do it. Every time I learned something new about Tammy, it persuaded me to love her more.

What's a Pastor Jill?

One afternoon, we were walking through a mall doing some window shopping and ended up in front of a jewellery store looking at engagement rings and wedding bands. We hadn't planned to shop for wedding rings, but it seemed as though that's what we were doing.

Getting married had never come up in our conversations before, but as we stood there, Tammy turned to me and said, "If we're going to get married, I don't think I can marry you unless Pastor Jill marries us."

I was totally confused. "What's a Pastor Jill?"

"She's the pastor of the church I go to."

"I don't do church."

"That's okay," Tammy said. "We don't meet in a church."

Now I was even more confused. "You go to church, but it isn't in a church; you have a pastor but he is a she; and if this Pastor Jill doesn't marry us, then we're not going to be married."

"We meet in a community centre."

It seemed to me that Tammy had deliberately avoided replying to what I thought was the most important part of what I had said. Clearly her relationship with Pastor Jill was a priority. I don't know if I had ever met anyone who had that kind of value for a church leader. I'd never had any interest in church, and I could only remember going into a church building for weddings and funerals.

I was lost as to what to say, so I repeated myself: "I don't do church."

"I didn't say you had to go to church. I just said that Pastor Jill has to be the one to marry us."

I could readily agree to that at least. It wouldn't involve going too far out of my comfort zone.

After our discussion, we went into the jewellery store. After looking at a variety of rings, we finally found a set that Tammy really liked. I bought the rings knowing that my next step would be asking Tammy to marry me.

The Proposal

Tammy's children and I began to put together a plan for a surprise proposal. The first thing I did was tell Tammy I wanted to start the New Year engaged. I think she understood that I was going to propose on New Year's Eve, and that's just the way her kids and I wanted it. The plan was to propose on the morning of Christmas Day. One of the necessary accessories was mistletoe. After an extensive search in Calgary, we found out that no real mistletoe had been shipped into Calgary that year. We had to make do with plastic mistletoe!

On Christmas morning, we put our plan into action. The first part was gathering in the living room to open gifts and drink the traditional eggnog. Then I snuck out of the room and went into the master bedroom, where we had hung the mistletoe. I had previously hidden the engagement ring in the bedroom, so I brought it out. I knew Tammy would be coming into the room soon for us to have a cigarette together.

> I could tell they weren't about to allow me to propose without witnesses.

When she walked in a few moments later, she was followed by all of her children. Them being there hadn't been a part of our original plan, but I could tell they weren't about to allow me to propose without witnesses. I got down on one knee beside the bed, opened the box with the engagement ring inside, and asked Tammy to be my wife. Everyone in the room had tears in their eyes as Tammy said "Yes!"

Marriage Counselling

Pastor Jill had agreed to marry us, but one of her conditions was that she give us marriage counselling. I had no idea what that would be like, but I didn't think it would be too difficult. We arranged to have her over to our house once every couple of weeks for the four months before the wedding. I figured I could put up with it because I was sure I would never see her again after the wedding.

Each time, we talked about some of the difficulties married couples face and how we could overcome them. Pastor Jill instructed us on the proper ways to handle disagreement. Over the four months of meetings, she went through a long list of possible problems that could come up in our marriage and how the answers could always be found in the Bible.

We got to know Pastor Jill well during our meetings and learned that she really wanted the best for our life together.

Wedding Day

Our wedding day was June 23, 2007. We originally planned to have the wedding at the community centre where Pastor Jill's church met for their Sunday services, but that was changed when we found out that my family from Ontario would not be coming. My mom had suffered a stroke two weeks earlier and my sisters and their families decided to stay close to home. Because we wouldn't be needing the extra room, we changed the location to our own back yard. I bought a folding gazebo for shade for the wedding party and we decorated the inside of the fence with streamers. We borrowed chairs from the church, and after everything was set up we thought it looked great.

I spent the night before the wedding at Ervin and Byra's. When Tammy and I said good night and I left our house, we were both very excited.

The morning of the wedding, I found out that I had to pick up all the flowers to decorate our house and backyard. A friend had offered to donate the flowers, but he'd called and said he wouldn't be able to deliver them. I also had to pick up my

Our First Dance as Husband and Wife

suit, which was being cleaned and altered. I had forgotten about my suit needing alterations, so I had to race around the day before trying to find a dry cleaner. In the end, I found one at the last minute who could hem the pants, but not the jacket. In most of our wedding pictures, the tips of my fingers are visible below the ends of my jacket arms.

Fortunately, my buddy Dave and I arrived at our home just minutes before the ceremony was scheduled to begin.

As we gathered in the backyard, we began to notice dark clouds gathering. It looked like we were going to get blasted with a storm. Tammy seemed to be taking longer than expected to get ready, so I stood under her window and yelled out, "Tammy, come down and marry me!"

I didn't know at the time, but someone unexpected had arrived and gone up to see Tammy. A lady that was very dear to her, whom she called Auntie Mom, was with her, and through all the excitement they were having to redo Tammy's makeup.

Pastor Jill's husband, John, got my attention. "I hope she comes down before the monsoon hits."

The clouds were getting darker and the wind was picking up. If it got much worse, I thought the gazebo might lift off the lawn.

Finally, almost two hours late, Tammy came around from the front door escorted by her dad, Samuel. She looked fabulous! We forgot all about the delays and started the ceremony.

By now, the wind was blowing things around the yard and some of the streamers were coming off the fence. The rain had started to fall and some of us were huddled inside the canvas gazebo while others sheltered under umbrellas. Pastor Jill shortened the vows as much as she could, and we rushed our way through the "I do's". She said we could quickly pretend to do the signing for pictures, and then actually sign inside the house later.

> "I hope she comes down before the monsoon hits."

We got a few pictures and then ran through the wind and rain into the house. When we all crowded inside, Tammy, myself, Ervin, and Tammy's daughter Carrissa signed the marriage certificate.

Now it was time for some food and fun. Tammy's parents, Samuel and Dot, had been a great help to us preparing for the wedding. They were very supportive. When I had asked for Samuel's permission to marry Tammy, he had agreed but told me she came with a no-return policy. He reminded me of this policy just prior to the ceremony, and I told him this was one policy I would gladly abide by.

Dot had made all of the food for the reception, which should have taken place in our backyard but was forced inside by the weather. My friend Dave made the wedding cake. He had learned how to bake and decorate cakes while in prison. He was another one of my unusual friends.

One of the wonderful gifts we received that day was very special: Pastor Jill conducted our wedding free of charge. She told us later that we had probably cured her of ever agreeing to do an outdoor wedding again. We all looked a little dishevelled from the wind and rain.

> One of the wonderful gifts we received that day was very special: Pastor Jill conducted our wedding free of charge.

Later in the afternoon, as most of the guests left, the rest of us went back into the yard. The storm had blown over and it had turned into a wonderful evening.

We received another gift from Leslie, a rather unusual lady I had dated for a while before meeting Tammy. She had brought her new boyfriend to the wedding, along with two cases of homemade wine she had taken from her husband's wine cellar. We made a fire in the fire pit, had a few glasses of wine with our friends and family, and partied into the night.

Tammy and I went to bed around 2:00 a.m. Some of the others continued partying until about six in the morning. Dave was the designated driver, and he drove a few people home who'd had too much to drink. He also watched over the fire pit and made sure everyone was safe.

Out for a family dinner 2015

THE BEGINNING OF MY PAIN

chapter six

Hay and Horse Manure

THREE MONTHS AFTER OUR WEDDING, WE DECIDED TO GET A DOG. Tammy had some friends who had a ranch near the town of Vulcan, and they were looking for a home for their young Rottweilers. We decided to go to their ranch for the day and see if she would fit in with our family. We all loved having cats and dogs around our house. My friend Dave asked if he could go with us. He had heard that this rancher owned horses and he wanted to see if he could ride one.

I had ridden horses many times growing up, but I'd had some bad experiences. I had no desire to ride again. When we got there, they had a couple of young horses out in the corral; they were starting to break the horses to the saddle. One horse was saddled, but no one had ridden it yet. When Tammy's friends asked if anyone wanted to give it a try, macho Dave said he would. The first time he got in the saddle, the horse reared up and almost bucked him off.

These friends were hoping to get one of the horses calm enough for all of us to have a short ride, but these young horses weren't completely broken. The saddle was moved to the second pony and Dave tried again. Same result. He was no sooner aboard than the horse reared up and tried to unload him. Dave finally got down safely, and we all decided there would be no rides for the rest of the day.

Just then, one of the owners rode up on her older grey mare. She went into the barn, unsaddled her horse, and gave it some water. After we were introduced, we talked about the Rottweiler puppies. One of the workers on the ranch told her that some of us had wanted to ride one of the horses, but that hadn't worked out with the young geldings. She suggested we could have short rides on her grey mare; we would have to do it bareback because she wouldn't put the saddle back on so soon after riding it herself.

Some of the kids still wanted a ride, so I agreed. To my chagrin, it was decided that I would be first, although I didn't want any part of it. The owner said she would get on first and I could climb on behind her. She had the grey mare stand beside the fence and I climbed up that way. She held on to the horse's mane and I had a death grip around her waist.

Then she decided to jump off. I made a lunge for the mane and grabbed on with both hands. There I was, lying belly down on the back of the horse. I was terrified and the horse knew it. The owner encouraged me to sit up so she could lead the horse around by the rope. I was just looking for a way to get off as soon as possible. Then the mare decided it was time to let me know it didn't want me aboard. It began to bump into the fence with my leg pinned in between.

I started to climb off the horse and onto the fence, but everyone continued to encourage me to stay on. I was only partway off, so I decided to get back on and try again. I had just reached with one leg to get back on when the mare took off. My right arm got jerked after the mare, but I had no horse to land on. The force twisted me around in the air and I crashed sideways into the hay and horse manure.

Tammy was the first one at my side, asking if I was okay. One of the hired hands came over and grabbed me by the hand and tried to help me up. I screamed in pain.

"Don't touch me!" I yelled. "I'm damaged."

I couldn't feel or move anything below my waist. Everyone stood around, not knowing what to do. One of the help suggested they could put me in the back of their truck and get me to the hospital. Tammy and I said no and told them to call an ambulance.

> The force twisted me around in the air and I crashed sideways into the hay and horse manure.

While I was lying there, the pain in my right arm and back got progressively worse. I thought about asking Tammy to get me a joint, but I changed my mind. Then I asked if someone had some painkillers; the strongest anyone had was Tylenol.

The first help to arrive was the fire department. When they tried to lift me onto their flat board, I screamed again and almost passed out. The firemen had nothing available for the pain, so we had to wait for the ambulance and paramedic.

When the ambulance finally arrived, I had been lying on the ground in pain for almost one hour. The first thing the paramedic did after finding out I had no allergies was give me a shot of morphine. They pushed a scoop board under me from both sides.

Before they moved me into the ambulance, they said they would need to cut my pants off. I pleaded with them not to do that until I was in the ambulance. I said I would explain why when we were in the ambulance. After getting me into the ambulance, I told them I didn't want anyone to see that I was in the process of gender reassignment. The attendants' attitude towards me seemed to change immediately. They became very cold and business-like in their behaviour. Tammy got into the front of the ambulance with the driver and we headed for the hospital in Calgary.

Discharge

The emergency ward at the hospital was a welcome sight. It had been almost three hours since I had fallen from that horse. The emergency room staff began to investigate and record all of my injuries and prepare me for x-rays in order to further diagnose my trauma. They managed my pain with more morphine injections and other medications to stabilize me.

My list of injuries was quite extensive. I had suffered a concussion because my head had snapped back against the ground when I had fallen. All of the tendons in my right shoulder were torn and I had a rotator cuff injury in the same shoulder. I had fractured all four of the L1 to L4 vertebra. When I was finished in emergency, they moved me to a regular hospital room.

I was placed in a small ward with two other patients whom I noticed were women. I buzzed the nurse's station and asked them why I was in a women's ward. They said they didn't have room for me anywhere else. I told them they had to get me out of the room with other women immediately. I was legally a man, and I showed them my driver's licence which clearly showed that I was male. I don't know if they were trying to show their negative opinions about my gender change, but I didn't care. I wanted out of the women's room and into a private room, or a room with other men. I'm sure they were breaking some hospital regulations by putting a man in a ward with women. The staff finally agreed and moved me into a room with one other man. That only lasted for a couple of hours, and then I was moved to a makeshift room between hallways. I was given a tiny little bell to use to call for the nurse at the other end of the halls. I don't think the bell could even be heard that far away.

Every part of my treatment at the hospital was poor.

Tammy contacted Pastor Jill and asked if she would come to the hospital and visit me. I had been going to church very irregularly, so I wasn't sure if she would come. She was quite willing to visit me, though, and we scheduled a date and time.

The day Pastor Jill came to visit was also the day I had to undergo physical therapy, but I was sure the therapy would be done before she arrived. When I came back to my room from therapy, I asked at the desk if Pastor Jill had arrived yet. They told me that they had sent Pastor Jill away because I hadn't been in my room.

I couldn't believe they would be so inconsiderate. The staff did not even check my schedule to see where I was and when I would be back. This was the final event that convinced me I was going to leave. I told the nurses to call the doctor in charge because I wanted to be discharged. I made it very clear that I knew I could receive better care at home from my wife.

Tammy contacted a friend, and they loaded me into their car. At this point I was unable to do anything for myself, so together we began the two and a half years it would take to recover my life.

Depression

Before the fall from the horse, I was working as a truck driver and making very good money. When I went home from the hospital, I couldn't walk and we were living on welfare. I wanted to be responsible for my family, but I couldn't because of my injuries. I felt useless.

My future began to look utterly hopeless. A time of depression and despair set in that didn't seem to end. When I was younger, I had gone through periods when suicide looked like the only way to end the pain. I began to have those same thoughts again. All of my thoughts and feelings were consumed with my personal hell.

My family lived in a house for which we had signed a rent-to-own agreement before the accident. We couldn't afford the rent while on welfare, so we had to move. For the next two

> *All of my thoughts and feelings were consumed with my personal hell.*

years, I lived in my bedroom. I began to get fearful of leaving our home, or even venturing beyond the bedroom. Our family doctor said I was beginning to suffer from agoraphobia. I was afraid of any area larger than my bedroom.

I could see no good in my life, and I began to make those around me pay the price of my torment.

Morphine

The day I was released from the hospital, the doctors gave me a week's supply of Tylenol-3 for the pain. With all of my injuries, the Tylenol wouldn't even dull the pain. I went to see our family doctor and, after examining me, he prescribed a mild form of morphine. The morphine helped with most of the pain for a while, but after a couple of weeks I went back to see him again. I told him the pain was getting worse instead of better, so he agreed to increase the dosage.

Most of my days were spent flat on my back. That seemed to be the only way I could make it through without having to take more morphine than my prescription allowed. When I took too much, there would be a couple of days without any relief before I could get the prescription filled again. My entire focus was the pain and how to deal with it. I began to smoke pot again as a way to relax and handle the pain.

Within a few weeks I was back to see our doctor, asking for more help. He seemed to understand and quickly increased my dosage. This cycle continued over the next eighteen months until

I was on four different types of morphine with a daily dosage of five hundred milligrams.

One day I began to experience terrible cramps in my abdomen. I went to our doctor, and after examining me he said I needed to get to the emergency room immediately. One of the possible side effects of morphine use is constipation. The doctor said that my lower intestines were completely blocked.

When we got to the hospital, we had a chance meeting with Pastor Jill in the entrance. I had gone to church only a couple of times after our wedding and was a little embarrassed when she saw me.

"Hi Travis," she said. "John and I have missed seeing you at church."

"I haven't been feeling very well."

"Then church is the perfect place to be. People are healed all the time in church."

"I don't have any way to get there," I replied lamely.

Jill had a good answer for all my bad excuses. "There is a couple in the church who would gladly pick you up on Sunday and give you a ride."

I was out of excuses, so I agreed to be picked up the next Sunday.

After the examination in emergency, I was given a large bottle of fluid to drink over the next twenty-four hours. It was guaranteed to clean me out. Over the next day, I was in the bathroom more than the bedroom.

Flat-Lining

My family was still living on welfare in 2009, and I was slowly improving. Tammy and I delivered papers to make a little extra money. The hour or so on my feet each day was about the limit of what I could endure. We used a truck borrowed from Dave. I did the driving and Tammy walked and delivered the papers. Many times she would come back to the truck and find me asleep; at night I woke up every fifteen minutes and couldn't get a good night's sleep.

I went to our family doctor and he made an appointment for me to go to a clinic that provided overnight sleep tests. For the first part of the test, they sent me home with a small machine that monitored my sleep cycles. When I returned with that machine, they told me I had stopped breathing up to one hundred and fifty times per hour. The next step was to spend one night at the clinic, and they monitored all my physical functions while I slept. It was a terrible night because they would wake me up every fifteen to twenty minutes; I continually stopped breathing and the heart monitor would flat-line. I was diagnosed with narcotic-induced sleep apnea.

Because I had been on high doses of morphine for a couple of years, the functions in my brain stem that control respiration were beginning to break down. When I would fall asleep, I would stop breathing and wake up gasping for air. I couldn't sleep longer than fifteen or twenty minutes at a time, so I never had any restful deep sleep. The clinic recommended that I be fitted for a CPAP machine that provided positive air pressure through a mask to help me breathe while sleeping.

Before I could be fitted for the CPAP, I had some dental surgery and then caught a serious case of the flu. I couldn't eat or drink anything; nothing would stay down. I was unable to take any of my medications, so what started out as a case of the flu ended up in morphine withdrawal. Tammy had to take me to the doctor every morning for an injection of Gravol. That allowed me to drink Ensure, my only nutrition for a number of weeks.

> There were long bouts of nausea and vomiting, and I lost control of all my bodily functions for long periods of time.

Because I was a heavy user of morphine, it took seven full weeks for me to fully recover from all the withdrawal symptoms. I spent most of that time either in our bedroom or in the bathroom. I suffered extreme chills and shakes, and even hot flashes. There were long bouts of nausea and vomiting, and I lost control of all my bodily functions for long periods of time. My wife spent many hours cleaning up after me.

When the worst was finally over, I returned to the sleep clinic and was retested regarding the sleep apnea. They discovered that my night breathing had almost returned to normal. I no longer required the CPAP machine.

After the morphine withdrawal and returning to quality sleep, my life began to feel normal again. I wanted to be a part of my family's life, including going to church.

THE BEGINNING OF MY HOPE

chapter seven

Kelvin

ONE SUNDAY AS I WAS LEAVING CHURCH, ONE OF THE SINGLE GUYS came up to me and said he wanted to talk. I had talked to him a little, but I didn't know him well. His name was Kelvin and he began to tell me about some upcoming special meetings taking place at the church. It was a lot of effort for me to get to church once a week, and I didn't want to deal with the extra pain more trips would cause. It was a big deal for my family to bring me to church, especially when I needed to take the wheelchair. I told him that I didn't want to go to any meetings.

Kelvin began insisting and told me that I had to go to these meetings. He wasn't telling me that he wanted me to go; he was saying that I had to go. Normally, I would have told him I wasn't interested and asked him to leave me alone, but he made it very clear that he somehow knew I must attend these meetings. The final point that persuaded me to agree was his offer to pay my registration. I knew he didn't have a lot of money, and I could see this was very important to him.

The format of the meetings included an hour of teaching, followed by the attendees breaking into small groups of five or six people. I didn't understand much of what was taught, and I felt very self-conscious throughout the small group portion. In the small groups, we were instructed how to put into practice what we had learned. Part of this involved praying for each other. Sometimes when people were being prayed for, they would seem to pass out and fall to the floor. A person would stand behind them and catch them so they wouldn't land too hard. I couldn't figure out what was happening, but the one being prayed for seemed to feel better after the prayer or talked about something God had said to them.

Soon it was my turn. I stood up with my canes, but I was very unstable. I knew I couldn't stand for a long time before needing to sit down again. Someone stood behind me, but I turned to him and said, "I'm not going to fall." I thought that if I fell, it would probably cause more injury to my already bad back.

"Don't worry," he said. "I'm here to catch you."

I looked at him again and said a little louder, "I'm not going to fall!"

"You don't need to worry. I will catch you."

"I am *not* going to fall."

"Don't worry," he said again, casually. "I will catch you."

I gave up talking to him as the others began to pray for me. They told me that I should express to God what I wanted. I had never prayed for anything in my life before, and I had no idea what to say.

"God," I began, "if You are real, give me a sample of what You've got."

Then I fell. I don't know if the man behind me caught me or not. From the time I prayed to when I woke up on the floor, I remember nothing. When I woke up, they were all standing around and looking down. Some were still praying while others had worried looks on their faces.

> "God," I began, "if You are real, give me a sample of what You've got."

"How do you feel?" someone asked.

"I don't know." I began what I thought would be the long and painful process of getting back to my chair. I quickly realized I could move much better than I could a few moments earlier. Then I became aware of the fact that I had no pain in my back. For the first time in over three years, I was pain-free.

When I told everyone, they went wild. I had known some of them for a few months, and already I thought they were a little strange, but now I knew they were crazy. Some of them shouted and clapped while others just sat there and cried. They couldn't seem to decide whether to be happy or sad.

When I got to my feet, I could walk without my canes—and without pain. Well, this started the shouting and crying all over again. As I walked around, I felt the area in my back where the pain had been, but now there was no discomfort at all. As we continued with the balance of the meeting that evening, I was able to walk without my canes.

The meeting soon ended, and I stood to leave. I almost fell to the floor, because the pain returned the moment I walked out the door. I had to go back to using my canes to get home. I couldn't understand why the pain had completely gone for a couple of hours only to return.

Over the next couple of days, I thought about what had happened. I knew I had experienced something real, and I wanted to find out more. Rather than getting down about the pain returning, I was determined to find a way to be free from the pain permanently.

Pastor John

I had been going to church on and off for about a year, and was getting to know some of the people quite well. It never seemed to matter what kind of mood I was in; most of the church was friendly and cared about me and my family. One of the kindest people was Pastor Jill's husband, John. John didn't seem to have much to do with the Sunday service, but he would always come around and say hello. He showed concern for whatever was happening in our lives. He regularly asked me to join the men on Saturday mornings for Bible study.

My physical abilities were slowly improving, and my need of the wheelchair decreasing. I walked with a cane most of the time, and my stamina was limited. I had become a regular user of medical marijuana as a means of controlling my constant back and shoulder pain. I continued to use morphine occasionally, when the pain was severe.

I decided to check out the Saturday morning study group. I usually enjoyed the Sunday morning message, but I thought Saturday morning might be different—a good opportunity to hang around other men. I was sure none of the men knew of my gender reassignment, and I wanted to keep it that way.

I began to go regularly, and each time we were done I would go out to my truck afterward and smoke a joint. I always had one ready-made in the truck. A couple of times, John asked me to join some of the guys for breakfast after the study.

One week, I accepted the invitation to go with them for breakfast. When the group was over, I went out to my truck and lit up my joint like usual. I was about half done when I realized I had agreed to go for breakfast. I quickly put it out and began to look around for something to hide the odour. I found half an old cigarette and smoked that, hoping it would mask the marijuana smell.

> I found half an old cigarette and smoked that, hoping it would mask the marijuana smell.

When I got to the restaurant, I saw there was only one place left to sit, squeezed into a booth right beside Pastor John. They didn't show any indication that they knew I'd been smoking pot on the way to breakfast. I found out later they all knew right away. We had a good time visiting, and after we were finished Pastor John bought my breakfast.

Water Baptism

A couple of times each year, the church held Bible studies on Thursday nights for six to eight weeks. We had two or three different groups with various subjects, and people could go to the group that interested them.

I decided to attend a study intended for new believers. There were usually about fifteen people. Some had been saved for a long time, and others were newer Christians like me. It was interesting and helpful to hear how others lived their lives as believers. The leaders of the group allowed lots of discussion time.

One night, the topic was water baptism. We talked about what it means and why we would want to be baptised. Some people in the group shared about being baptised in the Bow River in Calgary. After reading about the baptism of Jesus in the Jordon River by John the Baptist, I felt in my heart that I wanted a river baptism. The church had an annual picnic and baptism at a local park beside the river. I decided that was where I would be baptised.

One of the leaders mentioned that it was important for new Christians to be water baptised as soon as possible. He seemed to be saying that a person wasn't really saved until he or she were water baptised. This confused me, because I had also been told that asking Jesus into my heart had saved me. Now I wasn't sure what to believe.

Over the next couple of weeks, the leaders began to make plans to have a water baptism service in the church. It was still early in the spring, so it looked like I wouldn't have the opportunity for a river baptism. It didn't feel like it was the right time for me to be baptised, but the group leaders persuaded me to go ahead with it. We had the baptism in a blue plastic tub in the church during a regular Sunday service.

I was still in a wheelchair part of the time and could walk with canes for short distances. People helped me into the tub, and then out again after I was immersed. There was some excitement around me after I was baptised, but I didn't experience anything. I was even more confused now. I thought I had done what I needed to do, but I didn't feel like anything had changed in my heart.

I decided to talk to Pastor Jill about my confusion.

A few weeks later, I had a meeting with Pastor Jill in her office. I told her about my confusion over water baptism. I hadn't really wanted to be baptised in the church, but I had decided to follow the direction the group leaders had given us. What I'd done was taking me in one direction, but my heart was leading me in another.

> God always leads us through our hearts.

The first thing she told me is something I will always remember: as believers we must always follow our heart. God always leads us through our hearts. He wants us to be responsible for our own lives, so we need to know His voice for ourselves. We cannot follow what others think we should do because they won't always know what's right for our lives. This leads to blaming others for every problem we face.

She told me that I could still be water baptised in the river during the church picnic, if that's what I wanted. It was all right to be baptized more than once. She reminded me that I needed to follow what my heart was telling me to do. She also recommended that I get some good scriptural teaching about what water baptism represents.

Instruction

Since Pastor Jill was one of the few people I had ever heard teach the Bible, I asked her for some instruction about water baptism. She agreed to get together with me a couple of times. I decided that I really needed to follow what my heart was telling me to do and be baptised in the river at the summer church picnic.

Water baptism is only a dead ritual unless we believe the truth about what it represents.

> *We were buried therefore with him by baptism into death, in order that, just as Christ was raised from the dead by the glory of the Father, we too might walk in newness of life.*
> —Romans 6:4, ESV

We began by looking at what the Bible says about water baptism. When a believer is immersed in water, it is a symbol of what actually happens when we're born again. When Jesus died and was buried, I died with Him. That truth is difficult to comprehend. How is it possible for me to be alive now, but to have died more than two thousand years ago with Jesus? I don't need to understand how God did it; my part is to believe He has done it. I was together with Jesus when He died, and I was together with Jesus when He was raised from the dead. These are the two parts of water baptism; going down into the water demonstrates me dying with Jesus and coming up out of the water illustrates my being raised from the dead with Him.

Jesus said in the gospel of John that *"unless one is born again, he cannot see the kingdom of God"* (John 3:3, ESV). I died with Jesus, and I've been born again to a new life in Him.

> *I died with Jesus, and I've been born again to a new life in Him.*

Pastor Jill taught me to look at something beyond the water and the actions. She told me to believe in something greater than what I could see. When I was baptised, I was to expect to receive from the new life that is mine now because of what Jesus had done for me.

Back to Montreal

Just before Christmas 2009, I headed back to Montreal to get a prosthetic testicular implant. This operation went remarkably well in comparison with some of my previous surgeries.

After a few days in recovery, I spent three days in Hamilton with my sister Selena and her family. I had a great visit with my sisters and the rest of their families. It seemed like my family was becoming comfortable with the changes in my life. My sister Jamie appeared to accept me as a man, because she gave me a David

Beckham cologne set for Christmas. I have kept that gift since then and used it sparingly, only on special occasions. I open it occasionally just to smell it.

On July 8, 2010, I once again flew to Montreal, anticipating that this would be the last surgery associated with my change. I also hoped this surgery would give me the ability to consummate my marriage. It would finish the process of changing who I was on the outside to agree with who I always had been on the inside.

> It would finish the process of changing who I was on the outside to agree with who I always had been on the inside.

This time, the operation was relatively short, and after a similarly short recovery time I boarded a flight home.

I didn't know it then, but I was going to require one more operation.

THE BEGINNING OF MY DELIVERANCE

chapter eight

River Baptism

THE DAY I HAD BEEN LOOKING FORWARD TO FINALLY ARRIVED. THE date was August 15, 2010. It was a beautiful sunny day for the picnic and river baptism. After a church service in the park, we all had a great time visiting friends at the picnic. Pastor Jill then gave some instructions about water baptism. Once again, I heard about what I should believe during and after my baptism. I very much wanted this to be the end of my old life and the beginning of my new life.

As we made our way along the path to the river, I really believed I had reached a point in my life of no return. I believed in my heart that this was where I would leave my old life behind.

When we got to the river, Pastor Jill and a couple of men from the church walked into the water until it was just above their knees. Jill asked the first person being baptised to walk out and join them. She asked them if they knew Jesus as their Lord and Saviour. When they answered "Yes," the two men lowered the person under the water and brought them back up again. There was a lot of cheering and clapping from all of us still on the riverbank.

After a few more people were baptised, my turn came. As I walked into the water, I knew this was the beginning of a new life. Pastor Jill asked me if I knew Jesus as my Lord and Saviour. I said that I did, and the two men leaned me back, and I went under the water. I believed this was the end of my old life.

They brought me out from under the water. I came up with my arms forward and felt like I was reaching for something. I looked down into the river and saw small black snakes leaving my body. Some months later, I asked Pastor Jill and other people who were there if they had seen them, but no one had. I just know that I had a wonderful feeling of freedom and peace after they were gone. I knew that I was free from my old life.

> *I believed this was the end of my old life.*

I made my way back to the shore and joined Tammy and our kids watching and celebrating. Her son Dustin came up beside me and asked if he could get baptised, too. I said that he certainly could. I walked with him back to Pastor Jill and watched him be baptised. Tammy's daughter Angela also got baptised that afternoon. We had a wonderful time, as many other people we knew and loved were baptised.

Later, as we made our way back along the path, Tammy and I walked together and talked about what had happened. Dustin walked behind us; he had a long, thin stick which he was using to irritate me. Every few seconds he would flick my ear or my head with the stick. It was funny the first couple of times, but it slowly became annoying. Everyone else thought it was hilarious, but I decided it was time to turn the tables on him. I reached up and pulled the end of the stick, snatching it away from him. He suddenly realized my intentions and took off running with me in hot pursuit. Being much younger, he had no trouble successfully avoiding my attempts at retribution.

Suddenly, I came to a complete stop, realizing that I was running, something I had been unable to do for almost three years. Walking without canes had been a real challenge for much of the last two years. I was thrilled with what I was experiencing and lifted both of my arms above my head. I shouted, "Praise the Lord!"

I was amazed. Since my fall from the horse in September 2007, I had never lifted my right hand higher than my shoulder. The fall had torn the cartilage in my shoulder. I was now able to fully lift my arms without pain. I began praising the Lord all over again.

Delivered

Three days after the water baptism, I went out on the balcony at the back of our bedroom to have my regular pipe of weed. I had been smoking dope regularly since the fall; it was part of my daily routine.

I sat down in the warm sun and packed the pipe. When I started to light up, I had an unusual thought. It seemed like someone quietly said to me, "Why are you doing that?" I stopped and let the lighter extinguish. It felt odd to question something I had needed for such a long time.

I put the pipe to my lips and prepared to light it again. No sooner was the lighter approaching the pipe bowl than I again heard, "Why are you doing that?" It seemed more forceful this time. I looked around the deck and in the backyard, thinking someone was pulling a practical joke on me.

One more time, I started to light the pipe. "WHY ARE YOU DOING THAT?"

This time, I nearly fell out of my chair. It felt like someone was standing beside me and yelling in my ear. I stopped for a moment and began to think about what I was doing.

At that moment, Tammy came out on the deck and looked at me. I must have appeared startled because she said, "You're white as a sheet. What's the matter?"

"I just heard someone ask me three times why I'm smoking dope."

"Because it helps you deal with the pain," Tammy answered.

"The Bible says by the stripes of Jesus I am healed. I choose to believe what God says about the pain."

"Well, then it helps you to relax."

"But God says I am to rest upon the Lord."

I knew what the Word of God said concerning my circumstances and I wanted to believe Him.

I began to think about what had happened over the few minutes since I had stepped out onto the deck. What I had heard in my heart and my conversation with Tammy seemed to be leading me towards an end to drugs in my life. God was moving me to take another step. I made a decision right there to stop smoking pot and quit all pain medications completely.

> *Jesus was tempted in every way, and He has given me the same grace and peace He used to overcome His temptations.*

I know I was delivered from drugs that day, because I have never used marijuana since. There have been times, under pressure, when I've been tempted, but I've resisted the temptation. I remind myself what the Bible tells me about the freedom I have through Jesus. Jesus was tempted in every way, and He has given me the same grace and peace He used to overcome His temptations.

Three years later, we moved to a new home and found an old bag of dried weed and a pipe in the corner of the closet. To this day, we have no idea how or when it got there. Tammy and I had a good laugh as we destroyed those old memories.

The Free Gift

My life was changing so fast, and in so many ways, that I felt like I was on a ship being blown by a strong wind. I wasn't sure where I was headed, but I was thoroughly enjoying the ride. I was completely free of the wheelchair or any form of help to get around. I had been set free from all forms of addictive drugs and marijuana. I had become part of a wonderful group of people at church. I was enjoying my family and my life.

Everything I have ever received, or ever will receive from God, is a free gift. I knew that God loved me, and I knew that I had done nothing to deserve that love. God was working within me, and His grace and power was setting me free.

John 3:16 is, without a doubt, the most recognizable Bible reference in the world:

> *For God so loved the world, that He gave His only begotten Son, that whoever believes in Him shall not perish, but have eternal life.*
>
> —John 3:16

When I put my name in that verse, and made it personal between me and God, I began to understand that God loved me without conditions. God gave His Son Jesus long before I believed in Him. I was almost forty-one years old before I finally accepted the gift God had given me two thousand years before I was born.

The Application

Eleven days after I was delivered from drugs, I was asked to go with some friends to a cowboy Church in a small town named Claresholm. I'm a big fan of country music, so I was looking forward to going. The music was very good, and I enjoyed what the preacher had to say.

After the service, I had some time to talk to people and enjoy snacks and refreshments. At the back of the room, a table was set up with books and other information. I walked in front of the table and glanced at the items on display.

I stopped in front of a single form near the end. When I looked closer, I realized it was an application for Bible College.

"That's for you," I heard someone say.

I looked around quickly, but there was no one near me. I believed this was important for me, so I picked up the application, folded it, and put it in my Bible.

Later that evening, while talking with the pastor of the church, I asked if he knew anything about the Bible College and the application on the table. He said he knew about the college but didn't have any applications available. I took the one I had out of my Bible and showed it to him. He was very surprised. He had no idea where it had come from.

For the next few days, I thought about the application and the possibility of going to Bible College. I wasn't sure what I should do. My family and I were still living on welfare, so I didn't have the finances. The more I thought about it, the more impossible it seemed. Over the next few weeks, I gradually forgot about it.

Early in November, I received some good financial news. I had been communicating with the government over some disability benefits I had not been paid. They finally agreed to pay me what I should have received during the previous two years. This was going to be a great blessing for me and my family. A few days later, while reading my Bible, I found the Bible College application. I immediately realized that I was to begin the process of applying.

The regular semester had started in September, but they also had a way to begin first year in January. I set a personal goal to have everything ready to submit by November 24.

Part of the application was a four-hundred-word essay about why I wanted to go to Bible College. I really didn't know why I wanted to go; I just knew it was important to my life that I do. Every time I sat down to write the essay, I couldn't seem to think of anything to write. I was struggling with the thought, *If you can't write a simple four-hundred-word essay, how are you going to manage everything that goes along with college?*

A few days later, after I had helped out at the church, I came home wanting to lie down for a nap. Tammy reminded me that I needed to write my essay. I knew she was right, so I sat down at my computer and within fifteen minutes I was done. I still wasn't sure why I wanted to go to Bible College, but I was sure in my heart that was what I needed to do. I was beginning to see what God meant in Proverbs 3:5–6:

> *Trust in the Lord with all your heart and do not lean on your own understanding. In all your ways acknowledge Him, and He will make your paths straight.*
>
> —Proverbs 3:5–6

The next day, I called Pastor Jill and told her I was headed to the Bible College to submit my application for the January semester. She could now send them her pastoral referral letter.

When I handed in my forms at the college, I knew I was committed.

My memories of grade school aren't good. Most of my school years were filled with fights, suspensions, and moves from one school to the next. I also had difficulties with dyslexia, which made it hard to read. The thought of going to school again stirred up old fears, but I knew God wanted me to do this.

Voted In

One evening I had a bad argument with Tammy and decided I needed to go for a long walk. I got my coat and headed out with no real destination in mind. Walking and talking had become a way for me to work through my problems, so I walked and talked with God as though we were out for a stroll together.

After a while, I decided I needed a break, so I looked for a place to sit down. I realized I was at the front door of our church, so I sat on the steps for a while, wondering what I was doing there.

A few minutes later, one of the ladies from the church drove up with her older children. She asked me why I was there, and I told her I had just asked myself the same question. She told me that Friday night was youth night, and asked me if I wanted to help her set up. I helped set up chairs and prepare for some crafts and games. She and her kids then asked me to stay for the evening and participate. I enjoyed getting to know some of the youth in the church.

At the end of the evening, the leader asked all of the young adults if they would like me to come back the next week. Everyone put up their hand and encouraged me to return every Friday. It was wonderful to have a group of teens tell me they wanted to have me around. I guess I had just been voted in.

Friday night youth became an important part of my life over the next few months. I enjoyed helping where I could, but most of all I enjoyed hanging out with the teens. I quickly grew to know and love every one of them. They were all truly unique individuals.

After a few more months, I was asked to help with the fundraising for youth activities and youth camps. I had no idea what to do, but I wanted to give it a try. We began by having a bottle drive, which was very successful. Tammy then had the idea to make chocolates around Easter and sell them on Sunday mornings at the church entrance. That was a great success as well.

We began to see a greater number of youth on Friday nights, and we had enough money for activities. We went for an overnight camping trip with a cookout, which everyone loved. The youth all enjoyed themselves and began inviting their friends and family. Youth night was a safe place for them to hang out on Fridays.

One day, the leader of the youth group told us she wouldn't be able to continue her role any longer. We were all very sad to see the Friday night youth group come to an end, as I had become very close to them. I wanted to be a good influence in their lives, and I knew they were bringing growth into my life. These young people were filled with questions about Jesus and about life.

After the Friday night youth had been cancelled for a couple of weeks, the mother of two teens came to me and suggested we could work together as leaders to restart the group. We met with Pastor Jill and asked for her permission. She gave it willingly.

We immediately began getting together on Friday nights again. We started with our six kids and one other youth. Now I wasn't only a helper, but one of the leaders. We began the same way we had ended, by providing a safe place for young people to get together on Friday nights and have some fun with friends. It was lots of work, but I really enjoyed what we were doing.

After a few months, Tammy decided to get more involved and began coming with me. She had been working hard with the fundraising, but her being with me on Friday nights was wonderful. The group began to grow again, and within a few months we were up to forty youth every week.

First Year

My first day at Bible College was January 3, 2011. I had enough money for the first semester's tuition and book fees. Beyond that, I didn't know what I would do. Partway through the first semester, I applied for student financing to help with some of my expenses.

As I settled into the routine of classes, homework, and exams, I slowly began to realize that I *did* have a brain. I thoroughly enjoyed the class time and my interaction with other students. One of my difficulties was setting aside the time necessary to get the homework done. Many days I would go to the church after school, find a quiet room, and do my homework there. With four kids and Tammy at home, there were lots of possible distractions.

After each exam, I would call my mom back in Cape Breton and tell her about how I'd done. Whether my results were good or not so good, she always told me how proud she was of me.

I had always been close to my mother, but during my first semester I became closer to her than ever. She told me that all of her friends were kept up to date with her reports about how I was doing. Mom's words of encouragement were always with me, helping me through the tough times.

The Cheater

A few months into my first year, I was faced with a difficult choice. A friend of mine from our church was attending the same college. We had many of the same classes and travelled together most days. One day while we were heading to school, we stopped in a parking lot to do some final cramming for a test we had that afternoon. It was not a long test, but I had brought my study notes with me. We were required to write the names of all the books of the New Testament in order, with the correct spellings. My friend was looking at my notes, and then he took out his cell phone and snapped a picture of my notes.

"What are you doing?" I asked.

"Just making a copy so we can study the list at the same time."

We both read my list for a while and then drove the rest of the way to school. I thought it was odd that he would take a picture of my study notes on the way to school when he could have brought his own with him.

Later that day, we were both in the test room with everyone else taking the same exam. We were given our test papers and then began when the instructor told us to. I began writing. After a while, I glanced over at my friend across the aisle. He was glancing down at his lap occasionally and then writing on his test paper. He did that a couple of times before I realized what he was doing. He was looking at the picture he had taken of my study notes. My friend was cheating on the test!

I couldn't believe what he was doing. I lost my train of thought and all the focus I'd had on completing my exam. I stumbled through the balance of the test time, and when it was over I was sure I had done poorly. I was so focused on my anger that I walked out of the room in a daze.

One of the instructors must have noticed my expression, because he walked over to me and asked, "What's the matter, Travis? Didn't you do well on the test?"

"Honestly, I don't really know."

"What do you mean?" Now he looked as confused as I felt.

I looked around for a minute. "Can we talk somewhere private?"

We walked into another room that was empty.

"What's the problem, Travis?" the instructor asked.

I then proceeded to tell him everything that had happened, from my friend taking a picture of my study notes to looking at the picture while he was writing the test.

"I'm going to have a talk with the other faculty and then decide what needs to be done about this," he told me when I was finished. "If you can persuade him to come to us and tell us what he did, we may be able to prevent him from being expelled. This is a very serious offence, and if one of the teachers had caught him, he would have been expelled immediately. Do you think you can convince him to come clean?"

All I said was, "I will try."

Over the next few days, I talked with my friend a number of times and tried to persuade him to go to the dean of the school and confess that he had been cheating. He refused to admit that he had done anything wrong.

The instructor I'd talked to told me they set a deadline for my friend to turn himself in, but that deadline passed without any admission from my friend.

Eventually, the school administration confronted him about the cheating and he was given the opportunity to do make-up assignments and rewrite the test. He refused, denied the accusation, and never graduated.

THE BEGINNING OF MY TRANSFORMATION

chapter nine

Last Conversation

DURING MY FIRST SEMESTER AT BIBLE COLLEGE, I HAD TALKED WITH my mom every two or three days. I always looked forward to our conversations. She was convinced I had found my calling in life.

We had begun using Skype for our talks because it was cheaper than long distance, and it was nice to be able to see her face as we spoke. One day we made the connection but only the audio would work. We agreed to try again, but this time we only had video. I decided to phone Mom and tell her I would try again later. I couldn't get through on the phone at all. I tried a number of times, each time with an increased sense of urgency.

When I couldn't get through, I called the nursing home directly and connected to the nursing station. I asked them to please check on my mother immediately. I stayed on the line, and about five minutes later my mom picked up the nursing station phone. She quickly relieved my anxiety, telling me she was fine but neither her phone nor computer seemed to be working.

We began to talk about how our relationship had changed over the past year. I asked her to forgive me for all the mean things I had done to her in the past; I had taken her car once and sold it to buy drugs. She gave me her forgiveness and was able to laugh about it a little.

During this conversation, Mom told me about having tried to abort me. She asked me to forgive her and said that she was so happy it had not succeeded. We were putting an end to all the things we had done to hurt one another over the years. It was a wonderful time of healing for our relationship.

When I looked at my watch, I realized we had been talking for forty-five minutes. Mom had ended many of our previous conversations very abruptly because her arms would get numb holding the phone. I had an amazing sense of peace as we hung up.

Later that day, I related to Tammy about my long talk with my mom. I told her that it felt like it had been the last conversation I would ever have with her.

Celebrating Mom's Life

The week before my second semester of school, I got a call from my family in Cape Breton. My mom had been taken by ambulance to the hospital, and the doctors didn't expect her to live more than a few days. I was heartbroken. I was about to lose one of the few people who had stood by me through my entire life. My mother had always seemed to see past my crazy lifestyle and just love me. She had been my best friend through everything.

My final visit with Mom before she passed away. June 2010

Besides her family, the favourite thing in my mom's life was automobile racing. Racing of every kind, from stock cars to drag racing to demolition derbies. My mother never missed an opportunity to go to the races. She was sixty-eight years old, but her family knew that someone had to take her to the races when they were nearby.

On August 26, the staff at the nursing home where Mom lived noticed she wasn't her typical happy self. They called my aunt, who worked at the home, and she decided to go and see Mom. When she got to Mom's room, my aunt asked if she wanted to go to the races the next day. Mom replied that she was tired and didn't think she would go. My aunt then called her sister with her concerns, and she was instructed to call an ambulance immediately. She knew it was serious.

I flew home that same day, but when I got there

I was filled with hope for her, but I seemed to have lost all hope for myself.

Mom had already gone into a coma. I sat by her bedside and read aloud some of her favourite scriptures from the book of Psalms.

I talked to her and prayed. We knew from talking to the doctors that we didn't have much time left to be with our mother. I was at her bedside as much as possible.

When Tammy and I were married, I told her she would always be the number two lady in my life, after my mother. I had always been closer to my mom than anyone else. My mother was my best friend. I told her everything and she never rejected me or made me feel unloved. Part of me strongly believed I would want to die when my mom died. These were among my thoughts as I waited and prayed at her side. I couldn't see how to continue life without having my mother to talk to.

Three days later, the moment I had been dreading finally arrived. My mother passed peacefully into her future, and I felt my life shatter. I knew, without any doubt, that my mom was stepping over into a wonderful life with her Saviour. I was filled with hope for her, but I seemed to have lost all hope for myself.

Mom's brothers took care of most of the funeral arrangements, so Selena and I worked on a picture collage to be displayed at the funeral and reception. We had lots of fun with that, and also a few minor disagreements. Selena didn't agree with some of my choices for pictures. Any old picture that they thought was a little unflattering was immediately rejected.

We also talked about our mom's opinion of funerals. She always thought funerals were too sad. She didn't want a bunch of people sitting around, staring at her remains, and crying. She was all for everyone going to a bar, having a few drinks, and laughing over all the happy memories.

I was thankful for being fairly busy before the funeral, because when I had time to just sit and think, I felt lost and hopeless.

A short time after Mom passed away, I picked up my Bible and went for a walk down to the shore of Glace Bay. I sat on the rocks and spent some time thinking about how much I would miss my mother's love. My thoughts and emotions were in great turmoil. I felt completely alone.

I knew that the book of 1 John had much to say about love, so I decided to read there.

> *...love is from God.*
>
> —1 John 4:7

I know my mom had loved me, and this verse told me that all love came from God. It was God who taught my mother how to love me. If love is from God, then the love I received from my mom was also from God. I knew that God loved me, and this verse just seemed to make that love a little more real.

> *We know how much God loves us because we have felt his love and because we believe him when he tells us that he loves us dearly.*
>
> —1 John 4:16, TLB

My mother had told me that she loved me many times, and I always believed her. I was beginning to see that the love I received from my mom didn't come to an end when she died. I could continue to receive her love from the one who had given it to her. My mom was gone, but I was loved by God, who could never die. I was able to receive love in a way that would never change.

> *God is love…*
>
> —1 John 4:16

As I thought about God's love for me, it seemed like someone gently sat beside me, put His arms around me, and comforted me. I had been feeling angry at God about losing my mother, but now I felt His love in a very real way.

That love is truly unconditional. I had done many things in my life that could have caused my mother to stop loving me, but she never did. I had done many things that I thought were reason enough for God to have never loved me in the first place, but now I knew that His love for me had never depended on what I did. He had sent His Son Jesus to die in my place long before I ever decided to believe in Him. He showed His love for me while I was still far from Him. If God ever stopped loving me, He would have stopped being God.

> *If God ever stopped loving me, He would have stopped being God.*

I will always love and miss my mom, but I know I have a place to go to feel loved and accepted. Her passing could have been an uncontrollable time in my life, but my Father in heaven has filled me with His love and made me able to walk through the hard times.

Need to Know

I really enjoyed my life as a believer. I loved my wife and my family. I was part of a church family that cared about one another. My life was going in a good direction, because I knew a good God.

Very few people outside of Tammy and our family knew about my past life. I had told Pastor Jill about my life as a girl growing up, and as a woman. I loved my pastor and hadn't wanted her to find out the truth from someone else. I also told those I worked with in our church youth ministry. Even the leaders of the worship team, which I was a part of now, knew about my life before I became a believer. I was convinced that they needed to know my past. However, I didn't share my past with anyone I thought didn't need to know.

I'm not ashamed of my past in any way. I had been living my life and pursuing happiness with all the information I had at the time. I wanted my past to remain a secret from most people because I thought life would be simpler that way.

A friend from church one day talked with me about his desire to go through gender reassignment. I had known him for a couple of years and I told him some of the things he would have to go through if he pursued a change of sex. I didn't think he understood all of the implications of what he wanted to do. I had chosen gender reassignment as a result of a lifetime of turmoil and anguish. I didn't see that level of need in my friend's life, so I tried to persuade him not to go through with it.

I've talked with other people who were considering gender reassignment. I've talked with others who have already been transgendered. The truth I know from my own life, and from knowing the lives of others, is that gender reassignment is not the solution. It cannot bring about the change

> *Until a heart knows the love of God, there can be no peace.*

of life people may expect. The real need is to have a change of heart. Surgery and medicine cannot meet the need or fix the true problem. Until a heart knows the love of God, there can be no peace. Only a life that knows and lives in the new creation in Jesus can be truly whole.

The Threat

I didn't want everyone to know my secret, although I had told some friends. I thought I was protecting my future. I now realize I was only hiding my past. My life before salvation could only hurt me if I allowed it. Being free from my past was my choice alone. I was beginning to see how becoming a believer didn't cover up my past; being born again removed my past.

One day, I got into a heated argument with someone I was very close to. I don't remember what it was about, but she ended the argument by threatening to post my secret all over Facebook. I was instantly afraid of what would happen if everyone knew my past. I loved going to Bible College and working with the youth at church. I thought I would lose it all. I realized I would need to be proactive and personally tell the leaders of our church's organization, whom even Pastor Jill answered to.

Together with Pastor Jill, we informed this group of leaders. She didn't believe that my past should be a hindrance to my being a youth leader, or a part of other ministries in the church. The other leaders agreed and I was allowed to continue doing the things I loved.

I felt as if a huge weight had been removed from my shoulders. I loved being a part of the worship team on Sunday mornings. The youth group on Friday nights was growing in strength and numbers. My studies at the Bible College were having a huge impact on my life. I was beginning to see how rewarding life could be when I worked at being a blessing to others.

The Nuke

On February 20, 2013, the nuke exploded. What I had been dreading for years finally happened. While attending a meeting along with some other leaders from our church, I received a text from Tammy during a break. She said, "Your secret is all over Facebook!"

I walked over to Pastor Jill and told her. All she said was "Oh no!"

I had no idea what to do. Tammy wanted to do some serious physical harm to the person who had posted my past on Facebook, but we knew that wouldn't help. Part of me wanted to disappear; then I would never have to face the people at church again, but that would betray the trust they had put in me. I had become close to Pastor Jill and many others at church, so I determined to go through this the right way.

The next day, I met with Pastor Jill and her leaders. They thought it would be best if I temporarily stepped down from any position of leadership. In my heart, I didn't believe that should be necessary, but I agreed so that the situation wouldn't become a stumbling stone to my church family. We agreed that I would meet with the membership of the church after the coming Sunday service and share with them a short version of my life. Pastor Jill thought it would be a good way for the people to get my story straight from me, and to allow for some time of reaction and feedback.

As I waited out in the church lobby near the end of the Sunday service, I felt like a man about to stand in front of a firing squad. I thought about the possibility of my hopes and dreams coming to an end. I really didn't know what to expect. Before I went into the meeting, Pastor Jill assured me that most of my church family fully supported me—and she obviously knew her church family better than I did.

> *I felt like a man about to stand in front of a firing squad.*

I told them as clearly as I could about my struggles with my identity, both as a person and also in relation to my gender. I explained my journey from birth as a girl, growing up always wondering who I was, and then discovering gender reassignment. I explained the process of change, including the hormone treatments and surgeries. None of that brought lasting peace into my life until I met Jesus. The gender reassignment probably saved my life, but only Jesus could have saved my soul. I was always looking for a way to feel loved and accepted. The sex change had just been another unsuccessful way to find value for my life. I know now that all the hope and dignity I was searching for waited for me when I made Jesus the Lord of my life.

I was completely surprised by the reaction I received. There were a few questions, but the majority of the responses I got were loving and supportive. Most people said they believed my life before becoming a Christian was dead and gone.

I experienced a great deal of love and acceptance from most of the congregation. I knew there were a few people who didn't agree, but I contin-

> I know now that all the hope and dignity I was searching for waited for me when I made Jesus the Lord of my life.

ue to hope that will change someday. I had expected more of a negative response. The reaction I got made it clear that I should have been open about my past from the beginning. If I really believed I was free from my past, I should be free to talk about it. Since that day, I have had no fear about telling anyone about my past and how Jesus has set me free from it.

THE BEGINNING OF MY FUTURE

chapter ten

A New Creation

HAVING BEEN RELEASED FROM MY DUTIES AT CHURCH, I SUDDENLY HAD more time with nothing to do. I had been involved in many of the things going on at my church, as I loved spending time helping out wherever help was needed. I seriously considered dropping out of Bible College, but I eventually chose to stay. I realized that would just be another form of running away from my past. Even with school and homework, I still had lots of free time to think.

At Bible College, we had been taught that there were generally two methods of studying the Bible. One is called eisegesis, which means "to lead into." It refers to a form of study where a person may have preconceived ideas or beliefs and they tend to bend the Scriptures' meaning to say what they already believe. The second, and far superior, form of study is exegesis. It means "to lead out of." This is where a person searches the Scriptures in pursuit of what the Bible says and where it leads him. Such a person is willing to change his mind and believe what the Word of God says.

We were always reminded in Bible College that what we believed must be what the Word of God says. I began to spend more time searching the Scriptures to see what the Word had to say about me and my life. I want to be a positive influence for others who may be having similar experiences to mine.

I was born a girl, and I lived as a girl for the first thirty-one years of my life. When I was twenty-one years old, I gave birth to my son, Jesse. At the age of thirty-one, I began hormone treatments and surgeries that changed my physical appearance to that of a man. I am now married, and my wife Tammy is a wonderful person.

> *Therefore if anyone is in Christ, he is a new creature; the old things passed away; behold, new things have come.*
> —2 Corinthians 5:17

Of all the realities in God's Word, I think the new creation means more to me than anything else. This 2 Corinthians verse tells me that I am a new creation. My old life is dead and a new life has begun. Who I was and what I did before I became a believer has passed away. When I gave my life to Jesus, God accepted me just as I was, but He didn't leave me just as I was. He made me a new creation.

When the Pharisee named Nicodemus came and talked with Jesus, Jesus said to him, "You must be born again." Thinking of only natural methods, Nicodemus said that a person cannot go back into his mother's womb and be born again. We must look beyond what is possible in this natural world to find a way for someone to be born again. We first need to die to be born again. That's exactly what happens, according to the Word of God. Many verses in the Bible tell us that we shared in the death of Jesus. As I identify with and believe that his death was for me, the benefits of his death and resurrection become real in my life.

> *I have been crucified with Christ; and it is no longer I who live, but Christ lives in me; and the life which I now live in the flesh I live by faith in the Son of God, who loved me and gave Himself up for me.*
>
> —Galatians 2:20

This truth has changed my life, and will change the life of anyone who is willing to believe it. I was crucified with Christ. The person I was before I became a Christian no longer lives. I may have done some things in my past that will impact my relationships with other people. I may have broken some laws that could result in me going to jail. Those are all things that

> The person I was before I became a Christian no longer lives.

may impact my life in relation to this natural world, but my Father in heaven and my Saviour, Jesus, only know me as a new creation.

Here's something else I found that blew me away. In Jesus, I am not known by my race, by my place in life, or even by my gender:

There is neither Jew nor Greek, there is neither slave nor free man, there is neither male nor female; for you are all one in Christ Jesus.

—Galatians 3:28

Because I am in Jesus, God only sees me as He sees all believers: one in Jesus.

Hope

When I watched that television program back in 1999 called "The Invisible Transsexual," it seemed to offer a spark of hope. I thought it could be the way for me to become who and what I had always wanted to be. After all the operations and pain and recovery, my physical body looked like the person I was on the inside. After many more hours of meetings with psychologists and doctors, I felt that the hope begun over ten years ago was becoming real.

Being married to Tammy brought me a lot of joy I had never known before. I'm so thankful to her for being a part of my life and helping me through my personal hell. She knew everything about my past, but continued to be strong for me. There are times when I can't get along with her children, but most of the time I love being around them. Being a part of a growing family gives me a feeling of responsibility and belonging. They have all helped care for me at different times, and I want to be part of caring for them in the future.

There is something very real in the lives of the people I see at church on Sundays, and other times during the week. I know many of them have had a life just as mixed up as mine. They've done some things just as self-destructive, but there is a hope of a better future in all of them. I'm beginning to have some real hope in my life. I'm learning that hope for a better future isn't something I can get by changing myself from the outside. Hope must come from my heart, through getting to know my creator and the indescribable gift He has given me in Jesus.

I Am a Believer

All my life, I have been searching for who I really am. I believe that the heart's desire of every person is finding his or her true identity. Our parents tell us who they think we are, and who they want us to be. Siblings and friends tell us what we should do. The news shows us who other people are, and what they think. We see and hear from celebrities and influential people all the time. Politicians try to get us to think like they do, so they can win the next election.

These influences come from those who cannot possibly know what is best for our lives. All of these influences will, to some degree, have an agenda not for our benefit. The old song title "Looking for Love in All the Wrong Places" describes most of my life, and the life of most other people.

What would we do if someone spoke to us with only the truth? They would never tell us anything that could harm us. Everything they said would point us in a direction that is only good.

They would give us instructions for life and their sole purpose would be our success. Would someone like that be worth listening to and following?

There is someone with all of these characteristics. That someone is the creator of the earth. He is the creator of all that is good, and only what is good. Everything He has ever done is intended for our good. The greatest thing He has done is give His Son Jesus so we could have lives filled with His quality of life.

> *He is the creator of all that is good, and only what is good.*

When I heard that Jesus died so I could have eternal life, I believed it and received it. When I heard that Jesus died so I could be healed in my physical body, I believed it and received it. When I heard that Jesus had died so I could have peace in my life, I believed it and received it.

I am a believer.

One Final Surgery

Though the implant I received was intended to give me the ability to have sex with my wife, Tammy and I never used it. Early in the spring of 2014, I found myself thinking about having it removed. I began to realize this was something God wanted me to do.

I decided to talk to my pastor about this. He had taken over as pastor of our church when Pastor Jill travelled overseas on a long-term mission. I told him that I believed God was telling me to remove my implant. Just like Pastor Jill before him, he encouraged me to follow my heart.

When I asked Tammy what she thought, she told me that it was my body and I should do what I needed to do.

Over the next couple of months, I considered the situation. Then I began to have some discomfort in the area of the implant, so I scheduled an appointment with our family doctor. A series of appointment and consultations followed.

It all happened very quickly. By the following Wednesday, the surgery was done and the implant removed.

Some people have said that because I was born female and Tammy is female, we cannot have a relationship as husband and wife. Even though I was born a girl, I have always believed I was a man. After many surgeries, hormone treatments, and much pain, my exterior now reflects who I have always been on the inside.

I Love My Father

Stephen James (Jimmy) McNeil was born on May 28, 1940, and he went to be with his Lord on December 23, 2014. I loved my father, and I know he loved me. He carried my grade one picture in his wallet for almost thirty-five years. My dad knew all about my life; some things he understood, and some he didn't. That didn't change the fact that he loved me.

My father always made sure his family was provided for. We always had a warm home, and there was always food on the table. Dad may have been on the road much of the time, but we were always taken care of.

My final visit with Dad before he passed away. September 2015

During many long conversations with my sisters while preparing for his farewell ceremony, I learned how Dad had helped many people in our community. He didn't have much himself, but he was always willing to help others who had less. This was a part of my father's life that I didn't see when I was young.

Many times as I was growing up, my dad did things that I would get angry about. He didn't treat my mother very well, and he cheated on her continually. His way of life eventually led to their divorce. All these things cannot change the fact that I loved my father.

I love my dad because I will always be his child. He loved me because he will always be my father. Love is not defined by our emotions or our circumstances. Love must always look to something that cannot be changed. I can always be confident in the love of God, because He will never change.

You Can't Fix Dead

A couple of years ago, I was in a Bible study with some friends at church and we were looking at some of the truths in the Bible that had changed our lives. Most of our discussion concerned the new live we have in Jesus. The real good news is all about the death, burial, and resurrection of Jesus. The Old Testament is packed full of stories and word pictures that point towards the future sacrifice of Jesus for all mankind. Every Old Testament sacrifice revealed some aspect of the death and resurrection of Jesus. The life of Jesus, His death and resurrection, and the offering of His blood is the focal point of history.

As our group talked about being born again and becoming new creations in Jesus, we began to follow the steps in the death and resurrection of Jesus, and the fact that the Word of God tells us that we were there with Him at every step. We were with Him when He was crucified. Everything in my life that could separate me from God was put on Jesus. He suffered and died as my substitute.

> *I have been crucified with Christ; and it is no longer I who live, but Christ lives in me; and the life which I now live in the flesh I live by faith in the Son of God, who loved me and gave Himself up for me.*
>
> —Galatians 2:20

We were with Him when He died. When I believed in Jesus as my Lord, I received all of the benefits He purchased on my behalf.

> *Or do you not know that all of us who have been baptized into*
> *Christ Jesus have been baptized into His death?*
>
> —Romans 6:3

We were with Him when He was raised from the dead. When God raised Jesus from the dead, He could see all of us being raised from the dead together with Him. God had planned to do this for us from before the creation of the world.

> *…having been buried with Him in baptism, in which you were*
> *also raised up with Him through faith in the working of God,*
> *who raised Him from the dead.*
>
> —Colossians 2:12

We were with Him when He went into the holy place in heaven and was seated at the right hand of the Father. A man had brought sin into the world; that was Adam. A man had to pay the penalty for that sin; that was Jesus. He took His own blood into heaven and offered it as proof that He had died for the sins of mankind. Jesus has made a way for every one of us to become a child of God. He has always wanted us to be in His family.

> *…[God] raised us up with Him, and seated us with Him in the*
> *heavenly places in Christ Jesus…*
>
> —Ephesians 2:6

We will be with Him throughout eternity.

Then we who are alive and remain will be caught up together
with them in the clouds to meet the Lord in the air, and so we
shall always be with the Lord.

—1 Thessalonians 4:17

These realities may be difficult to believe and understand, but we need to realize that God's plans and methods are not ours. His eternal purpose has always been the same: He desires a family that knows Him the way Jesus knows Him. If we believe what His Word says and trust in the Lord with all of our hearts, understanding will grow in our hearts.

As the group discussed the fact that we died with Jesus and were born again, I realized that I shouldn't be trying to fix who I was before I was saved. That old way of living isn't a part of my new life in Jesus. My goal as a believer should always be the discovery of my new life in Christ. The wonderful future God has planned for me can only be found in Jesus. God's indescribable gift to me is to be born again, and to live my life as a new creation—because you can't fix dead.

HOW TO BE BORN AGAIN

Your past can't stop you from being all that God wants you to be. That incredible future can be yours by believing what God has done for you through the death and resurrection of Jesus. If you want to know and experience the love God has for you, please pray the following prayer. Say the words so you can hear them and believe what you are saying.

Father in heaven, I believe that You sent Jesus to die for me and to pay the penalty for all my sins. I believe that Jesus went to hell in my place and that He was raised from the dead so I could spend eternity with You. Jesus, I declare that You are my Lord. I believe You will instruct me with the Bible, the Word of God, and will guide my life by Your Holy Spirit. I thank You for giving me a new life as a child of God.

AFTERWORD

by Chris Schwab

My wife Marilyn and I first met Travis in 2009. He was coming to church in a wheelchair at the time and we would occasionally say hello or talk a little about how he was doing. Through other friends at church, we began to hear about Travis' progress towards being able to walk with canes and finally without any support. Over a short period of time, we saw a remarkable change in his physical and spiritual wellbeing.

The next year, we got to know Travis a little better when we were in the same Bible study. On Saturday mornings, we were sometimes at the same men's Bible study. Marilyn and I had also led a small Bible study that Travis attended for four or five weeks.

Marilyn and I knew very little of Travis' life until shortly before "the nuke" went off. We didn't know that Travis was transsexual until Pastor Jill told us. She made it clear that she had known Travis' story for a couple of years and continued to be a strong support for Travis and his family.

We let Travis know that we believed in him and that we thought he had done nothing wrong. It may have been better for him to be open about his life before he became a believer, but then we all have things in our history we have struggled with.

A few months later, Marilyn and I again began to talk about Travis' story being put into a book. We had discussed the possibility of this book two years previously at a writing conference. We strongly believed that his testimony could be an encouragement to any believer. Travis' salvation, and his life as a believer, is a clear demonstration of what faith in a risen Lord can do. The more we got to know Travis and his family, the more we believed this book was something God wanted us to be a part of.

Marilyn and I continued to discuss the possibility of this book for a year. In the spring of 2014, we took Travis and Tammy out for supper and asked if they would allow us to work together with them to write it. We are honoured that they agreed.

We began by planning to get together every Monday evening for three hours. We have missed very few Monday nights over the last year and a half. The four of us would sit on our deck when the weather was nice, or around our kitchen counter when it was not. Lots of times we just fellowshipped for a while before getting to work.

Travis would talk about his life and I would take notes. I should say that I *sometimes* took notes. Many nights, while listening to Travis, I forgot to take notes, so amazed at what he has endured and overcome. I constantly found myself asking the same questions I knew I had asked the week before. For the last two months, Travis and I did more detailed reading and editing, usually an additional couple of hours per week. Each week I tried to spend three or four hours writing from my notes and rewriting what we had reviewed.

Our next step was to send a copy of the rough draft to some friends whose opinion we valued and trusted. After three to four weeks, we got some quality feedback and then began the process of rereading and editing all over again. We also knew that when the book actually went to a publisher, professional editing would be required.

I'd also like to write a few words about something I've heard a few times with regards to Travis and his marriage. Some people feel that because Travis was born a girl and changed his gender surgically, he is still a girl in God's eyes and his marriage is a lesbian relationship. I have been told that it was God who made Travis a girl, and that cannot be changed.

In order for me to express what I believe, I must go back to creation. God created Adam and Eve and told them to be fruitful and multiply, to fill the earth and rule on the earth. God gave them authority on this earth. He created the earth and the physical systems that have been working in the earth since then. The strength and ability to fill this earth with man was placed in Adam and Eve at creation. The potential for every male and female child who has ever been born was in them from creation. That natural process decides whether a child is born male or female. We could say that all of mankind was in the loins of Adam from creation.

We all know there is so much more to the differences between a man and a woman than physical attributes. There are emotional and behavioural characteristics that seem unique to one sex, and others are part of the makeup of both sexes. My point is that what makes a man male and a woman female is not limited to one's physical appearance. I think we could all agree that the physical differences are a small part of our total makeup.

It is clear from Travis' story that he had an inner conflict from very early in his life. Tanya always felt like a boy inside a girl's body. The expression of his emotions was in a large part what we consider male. Tanya continually voiced an inner desire to be a boy. Do we say that is just a cultural and environmental influence, or could it be the result of the trauma of an attempted abortion early in his mother's womb?

Up to this point, I have only mentioned my beliefs about the natural part of the topic: what we can observe with our physical senses. What can we understand if we look at the spiritual part of Travis? What does the Word of God tell us about how God sees us all? The Bible tells us that man looks at the outward appearance, but God looks at the heart. The apostle Paul told us that we shouldn't look at one another according to the flesh. He said that someone who is born again is a new creation; the old man has died and all things are new. The new creation is God's solution for our past and His provision for our future. If our focus in this life is what someone has done in the past, we will never see them the way God sees them. As believers, we need to describe ourselves with the phrase "born again." We must understand that it's a perfect description of our reality. We truly died with Jesus and have been born again through the resurrection of

> The new creation is God's solution for our past and His provision for our future.

Jesus. Until we believe the truth of this wonderful new creation, we will always be limiting ourselves and others. Our heavenly Father has a fantastic life for each and every member of his family.

My wife and I have become good friends with Travis and Tammy through the process of writing this book. We have watched their lives, and the lives of their children, change through their knowledge of the love God has for them. The hard times they have faced together have made them stronger, because their trust is not in man, but in Jesus as Lord. We are honoured to call them friends, and to have their influence in our lives.

I sincerely thank you for taking the time to read Travis' story. It is a fabulous demonstration of the love of God and how faith in that love can transform a life.

For a more detailed account of Travis' surgical journey, and a way to follow Travis' life in the future, please visit our website: www.youcantfixdead.ca

ALSO BY CHRIS SCHWAB

Reality Check

Why are most believers living far below the reality we see in the promises of God?

I lived in that place for the first twenty-five years of my Christian life. I wandered from one struggle to another, seemingly unable to rise above my past. I could not see a future any better than my past.

Then someone pointed me to a truth in the Word of God that has completely transformed my life: the future I have always desired is already mine. Every promise God has made is already mine because Jesus is in me and I am in Him.

> *For as many as are the promises of God, in Him they are yes; therefore also through Him is our Amen to the glory of God through us.*
>
> —2 Corinthians 1:20

All my life I have looked in the wrong place to find myself and my reality. No subject is revealed more thoroughly in the New Testament than the reality of who every believer is in Christ.

Reality Check provides a look at the wonders God has given every one of us through the death and resurrection of Jesus.